Property Tax For Landlords

A Residential Landlords Association Expert Guide

By Steve Sims

Sebastopol Publishing

Property Tax For Landlords
A Residential Landlords Association Expert Guide

Published by:
Sebastopol Publishing Ltd
Gerlan, Pentre'r Efail, Harlech, Gwynedd LL46 2YG

Email for orders and inquiries: info@sebastopolpublishing.co.uk

British Library Cataloguing in Publication Data: A catalogue record for this book is available from the British Library.

ISBN: 978-0-99311695-0-2

About The Author

Steve Sims is a journalist and property professional. With more than 20 years in the property industry as a buy to let landlord, developer and holiday let owner, he is well-placed to understand the industry and the workings of a property business.

Steve was the author of the best-selling Understanding and Paying Less Property Tax for Dummies and has also written books about letting property, houses in multiple occupation (HMOs) and student letting.

Now, he delivers tax training for the Residential Landlords Association and writes books, blogs and articles for leading property web sites and publications.

With his wife Amanda, he also runs a specialist property tax consultancy.

They are based in the idyllic setting of Harlech, North Wales, on the fringes of the Snowdonia National Park.

His interests outside property and writing include West Ham United, live comedy, beer and music - although not always in that order nor one at a time.

Author's Acknowledgement

Besides the author, many unsung heroes work tirelessly behind the scenes to bring a book to fruition.

I would like to thank my wife Amanda for her knowledge and skill in checking out the technical points, as well as the staff at the Residential Landlords Association whose input was invaluable, and, of course, the proof readers and cover designers for their contributions.

A credit is also deserved by HM Revenue & Customs for referencing some of their worked examples and case studies.

The Residential Landlords Association

The private rented sector is regulated by more than 100 different laws, a number which is increasing year to year.

The Residential Landlords Association (RLA) was formed in 1993 to represent the needs of members before local and national government who make and interpret these laws.

The main focus is to reduce regulation and to improve property and management standards in England and Wales.

The RLA continually campaigns to improve the private rented sector for landlords and tenants.

Successes include influencing welfare reform, house in multiple occupation (HMO) licensing, buy to let mortgages, water charges and many more areas that have a direct and often financial impact on both landlords and tenants.

The RLA posts regular updates on current activities at www.rla.org.uk/campaigns.

How we fund our work

The RLA's work is funded from the support of members.

How we help landlords

Over the years, the RLA has increasingly become the respected go-to organisation for MPs, local authorities and the press to speak with authority about property matters.

Membership fees support the RLA's campaigning activities and much of the revenue is reinvested in membership services. In return for this fee of £79.95 a year, the RLA provides services covering all aspects of a landlord's day-to-day work. Many RLA

services are free or discounted for members. Discover what services the RLA have to offer by visiting the website, www.rla.org.uk.

Specialist Landlord Advice

RLA members have free and unlimited access to the Landlord Advice Team – one of the main reasons many landlords join and return year after year.

Our experienced team of specialist advisors can offer landlords much needed reassurance that they are receiving legal, honest and up-to-date advice.

Other membership benefits include:

- Landlord services - including deposit protection, referencing, credit checks, energy improvements and an arrears and repossession service
- Template documents - including tenancy agreements forms, letters
- Tax, mortgage and insurance assistance
- Industry updates and a regular magazine

RLA reader exclusive - 15% off joining

Join forces with over 18,000 landlords and become a member of the Residential Landlords Association.

As a reader of this book, we would like to give you a15% discount off your first year of membership.

To join, simply go online to www.rla.org.uk/join and use the following promotion code to activate your discount:

Your Exclusive Reader Discount Code
TAX15
To join, call 03330 142 998 or go to www.rla.org.uk/join

RLA reader exclusive - 15% off training

The RLA Property Tax Course is run by Property Tax for Landlords author Steve Sims. The course helps landlords understand how tax rules work and offers practical advice on reducing tax.

Landlord Training Courses

The RLA has delivered a wide range of professional training throughout England and Wales to landlords and letting agents since 1998. All courses are delivered by experienced and knowledgeable trainers at nationwide venues. Topics include:

- Letting, maintaining and marketing homes
- Small claims and gaining possession
- HMO's and selective licensing
- Universal Credit, right to rent and tenancy deposits

RLA members receive reduced prices. Book online at www.rla.org.uk/training or call 03330 142 998 (Option 3).

Plus readers of Property Tax for Landlords get an exclusive 15% discount off RLA training courses*.

Redeem the offer by using promotion code 'TRAIN15' when booking online at www.rla.org.uk/training.

Your Exclusive Reader Discount Code

TRAIN15

To book, call 03330 142 998
or go to www.rla.org.uk/training

*Terms and conditions apply: Promotion entitles those booking online to 15% discount when entering promotion code 'TRAIN15' upon checkout. Offer expires 31st December 2015. Excludes HMO courses, Selective Licensing, Legionella, Online Training course and Complete Letting Agents Course.

Contact the RLA Training team for more information, call 03330 142 998 (option 3). This offer is non-transferable and non-negotiable.

Foreword

Every landlord wants to maximise their profits. An important part of that process is to minimise the tax paid on rental profits and selling property.

We all know that we have an obligation to pay tax on the money we earn, but few realise they can do a lot to reduce the tax they pay.

This book helps landlords and property investors get their tax affairs on the right footing and shows that planning to save tax is everyone's right as enshrined in law that has evolved over nearly a century.

The financial problems of celebrities and international companies attempting to pay less tax through contrived tax avoidance schemes have hit the courts and the headlines in recent months.

Let me reassure you, this book is not about aggressive strategies that will land anyone in hot water.

In this book, you are told what the rules are and how to run your property businesses to gain the greatest financial benefit without breaking them.

Taxation exists to fund the society we wish to live in, and the Residential Landlords Association (RLA) would never advise anyone to evade tax. However, that does not mean it is right or fair that you should pay more tax than you rightfully owe.

After all, you may wish to support your local pub, but you don't want to pay twice as much as you would anywhere else for your drinks.

The job of HM Revenue & Customs (HMRC) is to collect as much tax as possible. Although they are not in the business of cheating taxpayers into paying too much tax, it's unlikely they will help you keep your bill down by pointing out savings, unclaimed reliefs or allowances.

In the final analysis, it is up to you and any professionals you employ to carefully plan your finances and check that you do not pay too much tax.

FOREWARD

For many landlords, letting a property will be the first time they have been responsible for preparing their annual tax return.

Armed with the knowledge in this book, this year's tax return is an opportunity to investigate your own financial affairs to see if you have been paying too much to the tax man.

At the start of every year the RLA is inundated with inquiries from landlords trying to meet the January 31st self-assessment filing deadline.

If you follow the advice in this book you may well find yourself not only better organised as the deadline approaches but also looking forward to saving tax.

This book is not intended as a replacement for your accountant or tax adviser.

Its purpose is to help you work more effectively with your advisers so that you are taking full advantage of all the available tax savings. If you don't use your tax allowances, you are in danger of carrying on year after year making the same mistakes and costing yourself a lot of money.

This book has its roots in our best-selling RLA training courses.

Our tax courses run for a full day, but even then we do not have enough time to answer all the questions asked by delegates, due to the variety and complexity of tax law.

We decided to write this book to satisfy the obvious thirst for knowledge amongst our delegates and landlords in general.

We know there is a lot of demand for guidance as our taxation courses always sell out faster than any other courses.

The author of this book created our taxation courses and delivers them all over the country.

They are not an academic exercise but a rigorous and practical real-life guide.

This book distils the knowledge offered in our courses and gives you the opportunity to access the author's expertise at your leisure. Whether you have invested in a single property or are managing a large limited company with hundreds of tenants, you will find this book can help you.

Many people dealing with tax affairs for the first time might feel that HMRC and tax advisers seem to enjoy overcomplicating matters with incomprehensible jargon.

Here, we have converted that jargon into an easy to read and accessible format.

Landlords are investors, and we congratulate you for making the wise decision to invest in a book that will pay for itself many times over.

Furthermore, we would like to thank you for your purchase which will fund our continuing work to help private landlords.

The RLA is a mutual organisation which was established to protect the rights of landlords and buy to let investors.

Since 1993 we have been fighting national and local government for fair treatment for people like you, and that has included campaigning on taxation.

We hope you enjoy this book and we know that when you apply the information inside then you will become a better organised landlord who will save a good deal of money that would otherwise be paid needlessly in tax.

Remember, minimising your tax liability is your right as a citizen and a taxpayer, and if you don't use it, you will lose it.

Have a great tax year.

David Melen
Landlord and RLA director

Contents Overview

Worked Examples

WORKED EXAMPLES

WORKED EXAMPLES

Contents

CONTENTS

CONTENTS

CONTENTS

CONTENTS

CONTENTS

Introduction

No one likes paying tax, but most of us recognise we have to pay our dues to provide the services that we and our families need and use, such as schools, hospitals and welfare benefits for the needy.

However, that does not mean we should pay more than we should.

From conversations with landlords around the country, it is clear many property people do not understand how the tax system works and the part they should play within the process.

Some are victims of shocking advice from tax professionals who should know better and some are volunteers who choose to ignore or just pay lip-service to their responsibilities.

The aim of this book is to reveal all those 'tax secrets' which professionals like to keep to themselves so they can charge high fees while keeping their landlord clients in the dark.

There are no secrets. The tax rules are there for everyone to read and apply to their personal financial circumstances.

This book seeks to empower landlords to understand the finances of their property business and to explain in plain English exactly what they have to do to keep basic financial records.

Once you realise that accounts and tax are simply about building a database of income and expense transactions and then extracting information to complete tax returns for property owners, the task becomes easier.

How To Read This Book

This book is not written for you to start on page one and follow through to the end.

Instead, it's a tax manual or textbook for property people and is designed so you can dip in to find information on specific topics by using the contents and index to identify the knowledge you want to access.

Throughout you will find icons and cross-references to signpost further reading or online help on official web sites.

This book takes you through tax and keeping financial records for property people, with a focus on buy to let and house in multiple occupation (HMO) landlords.

The book map works like this:

- Decide which type of property business or businesses you run
- Identify the taxes you need to pay for running these businesses
- Understand the financial records you need to keep
- Build a transaction database of income and expenses for each business
- Extract the data you need to work out the tax you should pay
- Find out how to complete the relevant tax returns

Along the way, you will pick up tax tips and strategies to help you pay less tax.

Remember all the information in this book is based on current tax rules and case law - nothing here can be considered aggressive tax planning that breaks the rules to get you into trouble with HM Revenue & Customs (HMRC).

However, a caveat is tax law can change quickly as the government tweaks the rules or the courts reinterpret existing law. It's a good idea to check any tax strategy you adopt with a tax professional before making wide-ranging changes to your business model.

Understanding The Format

Signposts in the text are designed to help you find your way around the book:

- Headings and subheadings in bold denote topics

- *Italics* highlight key tax cases that have gone before tax tribunals and the courts

- Bullet points break complicated information into easier to digest nuggets

Finding Your Way Around

This book has four parts and a set of appendices.

Each part follows a theme and the chapters in that part of the book explore different topics that come under that theme.

The chapters are also divided into sub-chapters that break the topics into smaller chunks of information that include a lot more detail.

Glance at the contents at the front of this book, or the index at the back to find the information you are looking for.

Here's a breakdown of each part to help you find the information you want to know:

Part 1 - Understanding Property Tax

This part is all about identifying what sort of property business you run and the property taxes you are likely to encounter. We also look at some notable court cases that back the right to arrange your financial affairs however you like to pay the least tax - providing you act honestly.

Part 2 - Managing Property Finances

Everything you need to know about the financial side of your property business, from how to claim expenses, the importance of keeping good records, working out your rental profits or losses and how to fill in your tax returns.

Part 3 - Capital Gains Tax Basics

Capital gains tax basics, how to work out how much CGT you owe and strategies to help you reduce the amount of CGT you might otherwise pay.

Part 4 - Specialist Property Tax Topics

Important tax information for non-resident landlords with property in the UK; landlords who take in lodgers; property speculators and anyone considering setting up a property company.

The flowcharts are designed to help property owners identify the businesses they run, the taxes they should pay and tax returns that they need to complete.

The charts cover UK and overseas letting property, including holiday lets and houses in multiple occupation (HMOs).

What the icons mean

As you read this book you will see some icons in the left margin which are signposts to further information in other sections of the book or online:

Telephone - The text alongside will have a telephone number to call, which generally offers the contact details of an HM Revenue & Customs (HMRC) help line

Further reading - A signpost to another chapter or page in the book where you can find extra information about the topic

Hyperlink - An address to go online to read or download more information. These were all correct at the time of publication, but the HMRC is currently moving to the combined government web site at www.gov.uk, so some links may change without warning

Calculator - Tells you that the text alongside contains a formula for calculating tax or a worked example. This book has more than 60 formulas and worked examples

Tick box - A point to consider in the action list at the end of each chapter

Important court cases - These are points of law that offer guidance over tax issues

The Action List

You'll find an action list at the end of each chapter. The list will offer some tax saving tips and strategies distilled from the information you have just read.

Sometimes, the list will prompt you to go on line or look somewhere else in this book for extra reading.

Who This Book Was Written For

This book was written with certain property people in mind. Here are some of the assumptions we made about you:

- You are a buy to let or house in multiple occupation (HMO) landlord
- You probably have between one and 12 rental properties
- You are dissatisfied with your current accountant who is failing to give you the tax information you believe you need
- You probably have not yet organised your back-office accounting and tax filing systems because you concentrate on letting or buying more properties rather than your paperwork
- You suspect you are paying too much tax and want to know how to minimise your liabilities
- You probably think you run one property business and do not realise you need to separate your financial records to complete different sets of accounts for more than one business
- You are probably scared of capital gains tax because you believe your tax bill is potentially a lot larger than it really is
- You do not fully understand how to minimise your tax by claiming the right business expenses and capital allowances

If any of these people sound like you, then we have hopefully hit the mark.

Next Steps

Your financial future very much depends on you.

While reading this book, bear in mind that we cannot possibly give personal tax advice to everyone as each reader's financial circumstances and goals will differ.

The advice is generic and aimed at the landlord profiled in our assumptions earlier in this introduction.

This book fleshes out the detail offered in Residential Landlord Association courses on property tax for landlords, capital gains tax and property tax for companies.

You may find these day-long workshops held in different cities around England and Wales may help you make sense of your tax matters.

They are open to RLA members and non-members. Further information is available online at https://www.rla.org.uk/landlord/courses/landlord_training_courses.shtml

If the reception for this book allows, an updated edition with the latest tax changes and tips will be published each year, so keep an eye out for the updated version.

A word about tax advice

The RLA offers a property tax service. Unfortunately, due to professional standards regulation, neither the author or the RLA can offer personal advice without following 'know your client' rules.

Feel free to contact the RLA with general questions, but do not be offended if no one can provide personal advice. It's not that we don't want to, it's because the rules say we can't.

Part I

Understanding Property Tax

The first step in tax-planning for landlords is identifying what sort of property business they run and how income tax, capital gains tax and other taxes are applied to their profits. This gives a road map signposting which financial records to keep and when to file the appropriate returns and pay any tax due

Chapter 1

Property Tax And The Law

This chapter is about:

- Understanding your tax rights
- Buy to let is an investment, not a trade
- Proving you're a property investor
- Eight property investment indicators

Let's start by addressing the elephant in the room. Despite what politicians have to say about the morals and ethics of paying tax, the law says landlords – and any other taxpayers – are quite within their rights to structure their property businesses in any way which legally allows them to pay the least possible tax.

Tax avoidance is a myth. Taxpayers either arrange their financial affairs to obey the rules of taxation or they don't. If they don't, then that's tax evasion, which is a crime.

That revelation comes with a caveat – the landlord must honestly report income and expenses and not break any tax rules.

Our best advice is for you to act openly and transparently in all your dealings with the tax man.

Understanding Your Tax Rights

The key to dealing with HM Revenue & Customs (HMRC) is to understand your rights as a landlord and a taxpayer, then to exercise them to the full extent that the law allows to minimise the tax you pay.

Your rights were established in two important court cases.

The first is *Ayrshire Pullman Motor Services & Ritchie v Inland Revenue Commissioners [1929 14TC754].*

If you want to look up the ruling, the numbers and letters in brackets are the year the case was before the court and the case reference.

In this case, Lord Clyde made an historic ruling about tax avoidance that still holds force today: "No man in this country is under the smallest obligation, moral or other, so to arrange his legal relations to his business or to his property as to enable the Inland Revenue to put the largest possible shovel into his stores.

"The Inland Revenue is not slow – and quite rightly – to take every advantage which is open to it under the taxing statutes for depleting the taxpayer's pocket.

"And the taxpayer is, in like manner, entitled to be astute to prevent, so far as he honestly can, the depletion of his means by the Revenue."

In other words, taxpayers can organise their financial affairs in such a way to pay the least tax possible, provided they remain within the law.

Lord Clyde was supported by another landmark tax case – *Inland Revenue Commissioners v The Duke of Westminster [1936 19TC490].*

In that case, Lord Tomlin echoed the earlier ruling by stating: "Every man is entitled, if he can, to order his affairs so the tax attaching under the appropriate Acts is less than it otherwise would be."

The Ramsay Principle

Later, another tax case set out what has become known as The Ramsay Principle, which dictates what happens if tax planning is judged as tax evasion.

The case that set the principle was *WT Ramsay Ltd v Inland Revenue Commissioners [1981 STC 174].* The principle says if a taxpayer engages in a series of financial transactions that have no other purpose than avoiding tax, then the transactions are ignored and the tax due originally still stands.

In effect, this ruling returns the taxpayer to their original tax position prior to instigating tax avoidance measures.

Tax planning principles

These three cases lay the foundations for the tax-efficient organisation of a property business, which are:

- Landlords have the right to minimise the tax that they pay, but not to evade tax
- Tax avoidance should be transparent and honest
- If any tax evasion is involved, the Ramsay Principle is applied to levy the tax originally due

Buy To Let Is An Investment, Not A Trade

Landlords have to bear in mind for income tax purposes that although property business accounts are kept according to the rules for trades and professions, rental income is treated as arising from an investment.

So, even though HMRC call the activity a 'property business' and rental accounts are drafted according to accounting rules, letting property is not a trade.

"Trades" would cover businesses such as running a bed-and-breakfast.

A property business is a trade when the owner provides services over and above those normally associated with letting a home.

The difference between a property trade and property investment is the way they are taxed. Property transactions generate a lot of revenue and HMRC is keen to grab a share.

The simple truth is buy to sell is property dealing and a trade – so the profits are taxed as income. Income above the basic rate band is taxed at 40% for higher rate taxpayers and 45% for additional rate taxpayers.

Buy to let is an investment – rental profits are taxed at the same rates as buy to sell but the chargeable gain on selling a property is subject to capital gains tax (CGT).

CGT is charged at 18% for basic rate taxpayers and 28% for higher and additional rate taxpayers.

As a buy to let investor, you need to show your property is an investment so you qualify for lower rates of tax.

The definitive case law underlining this is *Salisbury House Estate Ltd v Fry [1930] 15TC266.*

The ruling stated that money from investments and trading are separate categories of income, and as such, are taxed according to the source.

The judge, Lord MacMillan said: "A landowner may conduct a trade on his premises, but he cannot be represented as carrying on a trade of owning land because he makes an income from letting it."

Another more recent case that confirmed this ruling was *Rashid v Garcia [2008] SpC 348.*

Rashid was a landlord with four rental properties. He claimed that because running the properties involved a significant amount of time, he should pay Class 2 National Insurance Contributions on his income.

HMRC argued that Salisbury House Estate Ltd v Fry applied and as his rents were investment income, he could not pay National Insurance.

Rashid's intention was to test the law to see if he could claim state benefits that were not available to landlords as he was not employed or self-employed in his property business.

The tribunal was told Rashid and his family spent around 20 to 28 hours a week working for his property business. This time included gardening, cleaning, maintenance and administration.

The court decided this activity was not enough to prove the case and that the work involved in running a property business was activity to maintain his investments rather than run a business.

So, however much time you devote to a buy to let business or whatever the size of your property portfolio, you will always be an investor, not a trader.

Proving You're A Property Investor

Every time you add a property to your portfolio, you need to show whether it's a buy to sell or a buy to let. Doing so determines the tax route you take for the property.

A buy to let is considered a long-term investment and certain indicators prove the property is not a buy to sell.

These include financing the deal with a buy to let mortgage and getting a rental assessment prior to purchase: a buy to sell is more likely to have short-term finance, such as a bridging loan and a surveyor's report indicating the likely sale price after refurbishment.

Of course, sometimes a buy to let is bought on short term finance pending refurbishment, but this does not make the property a buy to sell.

The key indicator for tax is the buyer's intention at purchase that is demonstrated by the presence of buy to let finance and a rental assessment.

Flipping a buy to let or letting a buy to sell

So you purchase a property with the intention of holding and letting for the long term. Then, a few weeks down the line you receive an offer you can't refuse from someone in love with the home.

Of course, you accept the offer – but do you pay capital gains tax or income tax on the sale?

This is where your intention at the time you bought the property becomes relevant.

No rules prevent a buy to let investor selling a property whenever they wish. The intention on purchase determines the way how the disposal is assessed for tax for however long the property is owned.

Because the investor had the intent to hold and let, the property sale is treated as a CGT disposal.

Conversely, if a buy to sell speculator decides not to sell because the bottom has dropped out of the market and he lets the property while waiting for prices to recover, the home does not become a buy to let but remains a buy to sell.

When the property is eventually sold, the deal is treated as a sale and is subject to income tax.

That's why proving your intention at the point of purchase is so important and why collecting evidence of that intention is vital.

See Page 78 – Property Register and records to keep

Eight Property Investment Indicators

If you are in dispute with HMRC over establishing whether your property transaction was a buy to sell or buy to let, it's likely HMRC will go through their list of indicators to try to prove their case.

These are the indicators:

Did the property investor work out the rental yield or sale price after refurbishment?

This is the primary indicator and a good reason why you must ensure you have the right paperwork from the start of your property business.

Was the purchase financed with a buy to let mortgage?

This can go either way. For instance a cash purchase doesn't prove the case either way and some buy to let landlords finance auction purchases with bridging finance and then remortgage with a buy to let lender.

Does the property generate rent?

If not, you will find it hard to prove that the property is

an investment. Unless you can show you purchased for personal enjoyment as a holiday home or had a charitable intention, like providing an uncommercial let for a relative or friend who may have fallen on hard times.

See Page 69 for more about uncommercial lets

How long was the property owned?

While there is no set rule as to how long you should own a property in a buy to let business, nonetheless HMRC would expect to see at least a medium term investment of 10 years or so. Selling within this time could trigger an inquiry into your purchase intention for the property.

Why was the property sold?

Good investors are continually reviewing their portfolios and looking at whether they can get a better return from selling one or more properties and buying others. Minute your business decisions, so that if HMRC comes back some time later to question your reasoning, you have the information to hand.

How is your property business organised?

HMRC naively assumes property people either run a buy to let or a buy to sell business. This is incorrect and many run multiple property businesses at the same time with different joint owners.

Don't let things drift, have a clear idea of your business structure, separate bank accounts, business records and clearly document your purchase intention for each property.

See Page 61 for more about running multiple property businesses

Conversions and refurbishments

Buying a property and modifying the layout to make

space for more tenants is often a sensible business decision that can increase revenue and profits.

However, redeveloping a property and then selling quickly may trigger a tax inquiry that examines your intention on purchase – was the deal really a buy to sell, not a buy to let?

Reviewing your decisions

Tax law changes quickly. Cases before tribunals and changes in government policy can undermine previous strategies, so make sure you are up-to-date with the latest rules.

These indicators should give you an excellent basis for assembling a portfolio of evidence of your purchase intention.

Action List

☑ Identify the type of property business you run – buy to let or buy to sell. Don't forget that you can run more than one type of property business simultaneously.

More about running multiple businesses and the tax implications – Chapter 3

☑ The documents and minutes to prove your a property is a buy to let or buy to sell should go into your property register.

Start a register for each property: document the eight property intention indicators with supporting paperwork and add details of owners, property use and capital expenses to calculate income tax and capital gains tax correctly.

More about keeping a property register – See Page 78

Chapter 2

What Is Property Tax?

Chapter preview:

- The main property taxes
- What is property
- Who pays property tax?
- Tax-effective property ownership
- Income shifting explained

Property tax does not really exist. It's a convenient collective term for a ragbag of bits and pieces of other taxes pretty much introduced ad hoc by various governments over the years.

Ministers find property investors are easy targets, because tax on immoveable property like a home is easier to establish and levy than tax on cash which is much more liquid and harder to trace.

Many of these tax loose ends were pulled together in two Acts of Parliament:

- The Income Tax (Taxation of Other Income) Act 2005 covers profits on rents

- The Taxation of Chargeable Gains Act 1992 deals with tax on any gain when a property is sold

The Main Property Taxes

The property tax for which a landlord or investor is liable is dependent on three main factors:

- The type of property business they run
- Where the property is located
- Use of the property

That said, most property investors have to tackle these taxes:

Income Tax

Landlords pay income tax on rental profits. Essentially, rental profits are the remainder after expenses are deducted from the income the business receives.

See Chapters 6, 7 and 8 for more about property expenses and calculating rental profits

Capital Gains Tax

Capital Gains Tax (CGT) is paid on the disposal of all or part of a property. This tax is charged on any increase in value of the property less some allowable expenses.

See Chapters 12-15 for more about capital gains tax

Stamp Duty

Stamp Duty Land Tax, stamp duty for short, is charged on buying or leasing a property. The rate is related to the property value

The current stamp duty rules for England and Wales were introduced in the Finance Act 2013, but Scotland has a separate set of laws under The Land and Buildings Transaction Tax (Scotland) Act 2013.

See Chapter 16 for more about stamp duty

VAT

Letting residential property is a VAT-exempt activity, which means landlords cannot charge VAT on rents nor reclaim any VAT paid on expenses.

However, if the landlord provides a service, VAT may be due on the service in the same way letting agents charge VAT for managing a property. VAT is normally an issue for developers rather than landlords and so is outside the scope of this book.

What Is Property?

Property is not defined in tax law. Tax law refers to 'land' rather than 'property' and the term is taken to include buildings, land under water, such as lakes and ponds, and any interests or rights in land, like leases and rights of way.

In this book, the term property means residential property, such as a home, a house in multiple occupation (HMO) or a holiday let.

The same rules also apply to semi-commercial property, such as flats or maisonettes over shops or offices.

Farms, industrial buildings and other commercial properties are often governed by specific tax rules that are outside the scope of this book.

However, tax law designates static caravans and houseboats rented out on long lets as property generating income for a landlord, bringing them under buy to let and HMO income tax rules.

Take care over caravans and houseboats. Just as a bed-and-breakfast is not letting property, caravans or houseboats run as a trade and offering other services are not letting property either.

However, static houseboats or caravans let on assured shorthold tenancy agreements are captured under the same tax rules as buy to lets.

Who Pays Property Tax?

The general tax rule is that the beneficial owner of a property is responsible for paying tax on any rental profits or chargeable gain.

The beneficial owner is not necessarily the person listed as the owner of a property at the Land Registry, but is the person HM Revenue & Customs (HMRC) will pursue if any income tax is due on rents or CGT is owed on a disposal of a property. It's important to identify the person or persons liable for property tax to ensure the right person pays the right amount of tax.

The rules are anyone receiving:

- £10,000 or more before deducting expenses from property in the UK or overseas

  OR

- £2,500 or more after deducting expenses from property in the UK or overseas
- Should notify HMRC of their income and:
- File a tax return for the tax year when the income was received

  OR

- Ask HMRC to collect their property tax by adjusting their PAYE coding notice if they are employed or a pensioner

Who is the beneficial owner?

The beneficial owner is someone who is entitled to the money if a property is let out or sold.

One area of confusion is when parents own a buy to let home but hand the management over to their children, relatives or friends. The managers may keep the rent in recognition of the time they spend looking after the property and the parents believe they owe no tax on rental profits because they receive no income.

The true state of affairs is the parents are entitled to the money and should pay the tax as beneficial owners. Just because they let their managers keep the cash, this does not absolve their legal responsibility to pay tax.

Tracking down beneficial owners

HMRC follows a formula to determine who the beneficial owner of a property which was established in the case of *Lawson v*

Revenue & Customs [2011] UKFTT 346 (TC).

In that case, the tribunal decided on a set of indicators to determine who has beneficial ownership of land or property by ruling they are persons who:

- Hold legal title
- Occupy the property
- Receive rental income from the property
- Provided the money to buy the property
- Received the sale proceeds from the property disposal

Another indicator is if they are named on a Form 17 filed with HMRC.

See Page 56 for more about filing HMRC Form 17

How many owners for a property?

A property in the UK can have four legal owners as a beneficial joint tenancy, but more as a tenancy in common.

Other arrangements, such as companies and partnerships, allow more owners, but we are discussing individual property investors in this book.

Tax-Effective Property Ownership

Making the right decision about tax-effective property ownership can lead to significant tax savings in later years, especially if one owner is a higher rate taxpayer and the other is a basic rate taxpayer.

When hearing the word 'tenant' in the context of property ownership, forget the meaning of 'one who pays rent' and replace 'tenant' with 'holder' – the term derives from the French 'to hold'.

Sole tenants have complete ownership, while joint tenants are co-holders of property enjoying the same benefits as a sole tenant.

Tenants-in-common hold a property together but may have unequal benefits.

Excluding trusts, companies, business partnerships and other complicated legal entities, which fall outside the scope of this book, individual property ownership in the UK generally falls into three main categories:

> **Sole tenant** – A single person owning 100% of the property makes all the business decisions and is the beneficial owner.
>
> The sole tenant is responsible for paying all the tax on rental profits or any chargeable gains.
>
> **Joint tenants** – Up to four people owning a property, taking joint decisions and splitting any rental profits or chargeable gains in strict percentages depending on the number of owners:
>
> - 2 owners – 50% each
> - 3 owners – 33:33% each
> - 4 owners – 25% each
>
> Married couples or civil partners are judged to split the rental profits and chargeable gains 50:50.
> Spouses can manipulate the tax they pay through income shifting.
>
> **Tenants-in-common** - This is the most flexible and tax-effective way of owning investment property.
>
> Each owner has a specific shareholding between 1% and 99% of the property which can be changed by a declaration of trust.
>
> Spouses can manipulate the tax they pay through income shifting, providing they own unequal shares of the property.
>
> This category of ownership does come with some drawbacks that property people should consider before embarking on a tenancy in common.

> If the shares are not specified, then HMRC splits the rental profits and any chargeable gain by assuming equal ownership.
>
> If an owner dies, their share in the property is added to their estate and does not pass to the other owners unless specified in a will.
>
> Furthermore, ownership cannot switch back to a joint tenancy once transferred to a tenancy-in-common.

Income Shifting Explained

Income shifting is nothing new. Accountants have shuffled shares in property ownership around for years for landlords as a key tax saving strategy.

The principle of income shifting is simple. Property ownership is split in such a way that when there are two or more owners, those paying the lowest tax rates own the greater share of the property.

Whenever you see two property owners paying different rates of income tax, consider this as a trigger for potential income shifting and a tax saving.

Income shifting can save property owners thousands of pounds in income tax and capital gains tax over the years and is relatively easy to set up.

Who qualifies for income shifting?

Any joint owners qualify, but there are some points to bear in mind:

- Joint owners who are not married or civil partners will pay capital gains tax (CGT) if they shift property shares around, so unmarried couples should establish tax-effective ownership as tenants–in-common when they buy a property
- Married couples and civil partners can change the proportion of their property ownership shares as they like without any impact from CGT

How income shifting works

Alan is married to Nicole and they own a letting property which returns a £7,500 rental profit each tax year. Alan is a higher rate tax payer (40%), while Nicole is a mum with a part-time job earning £15,000 a year. Nicole pays tax at the basic rate of 20%.

They have made no income shifting election, so HMRC assumes they split their rental profits 50:50.

- Alan's tax on his profit share is 40% of £3,250 = £1,300
- Nicole's tax on her profit share is 20% of £3,250 = £650
- The total income tax due on the rental profit is £1,950.

Alan and Nicole can make a declaration of trust before a solicitor that allows them to change their shareholding in the property to give Nicole a larger slice of the rental profits.

They decide to split the ownership 95:5 in favour of Nicole. They file a Form 17 with HMRC along with the declaration of trust as evidence of the exchange of ownership. Because they are married, the transfer is exempt from CGT.

This means Alan's share of profits decreases in the next tax year to £375, while Nicole's increases to £7,125.

This alters the tax they pay:

- Alan's tax on his profit share is 40% of £375 = £150
- Nicole's tax on her profit is 20% of £7,125 = £1,425
- The total income tax due on the rental profit is £1,575, a saving of £375 a year

Filling in a Form 17

Completing the form is quite straightforward, but a couple of points can catch people out:

- Give the postal address of the property including the postcode as the property description to avoid any confusion about the home in question

- Make sure the shares add up to 100%

- Make the beneficial interest in the property the same as the beneficial interest in the income, otherwise income shifting does not work

- The tax office must receive the form within 60 days of the earliest declaration date, otherwise the declaration will be ignored

- The evidence of the transfer of shareholding is a declaration of trust drafted by a solicitor – make sure a copy is attached to the Form 17

- If the shareholdings change, a new Form 17 and declaration of trust must be submitted

Form 17 points to watch

The optimum date for completing the form is April 6, which is the start of the tax year. If the form is filed with HMRC by June 5, the percentage changes take effect for the whole of the tax year.

Property owners can file as many Form 17s as they like, when they like, providing they stick to the signing and filing conditions and have a new declaration of trust drafted alongside each submission.

If the property undergoes mortgage and/or ownership changes, stamp duty is due on any transfer valued at more than £125,000.

You can avoid stamp duty by retaining your share of the mortgage while transferring a share of the property to a spouse.

Property owners can download a Form 17 from the HM Revenue & Customs (HMRC) web site [LINK: http://www.hmrc.gov.uk/forms/form17.pdf].

Separating The Money Out

Time and again, accountants and tax advisers see clients go to great lengths to make tax savings only for their plans to fall at the last hurdle by not finalising their strategy by moving their money into the right bank accounts.

A case that went before the tax tribunal that illustrates this is *Kings v King [2004] STC (SCD) 186.*

Confusingly, the tax inspector and the husband and wife involved in this case all had the surname King. Mr and Mrs King moved out of their home, which they owned as equal partners in a beneficial joint tenancy.

The property was let to tenants. Mr King made out the tenancy agreement in his name and had the rent paid into his bank account.

HMRC argued that despite joint ownership of the home, Mr King has assumed the right to all the money and was liable for the tax due.

As a higher rate taxpayer, he paid 40% on the profits, while Mrs King was a basic rate taxpayer who would have paid half as much tax as her husband.

The tribunal found in HMRC's favour, ruling Mrs King had transferred her right to the rents to her husband. Had the rent gone into a joint account, the couple could have argued they both retained control.

Even better, if the money was split between personal bank accounts in the name of each, HMRC could not have argued the issue of control at all.

Action List

If net property income is less than £2,500, landlords should contact their tax office to report the income on a Form 810.

This form is not available for download and must be issued by a tax office. To order a Form 810, call HMRC on 0300 200 3310

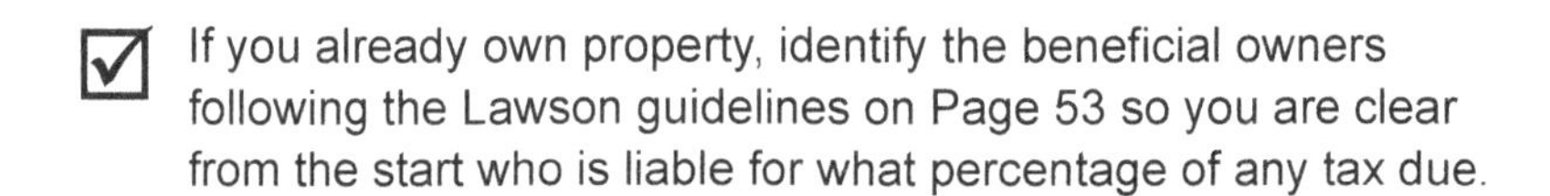

If you already own property, identify the beneficial owners following the Lawson guidelines on Page 53 so you are clear from the start who is liable for what percentage of any tax due.

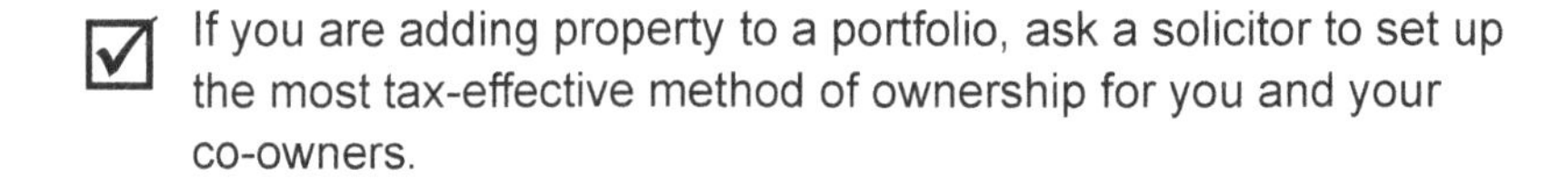

If you are adding property to a portfolio, ask a solicitor to set up the most tax-effective method of ownership for you and your co-owners.

Run the numbers to check if income shifting will save you tax - and don't forget that income shifting also affects capital gains tax.

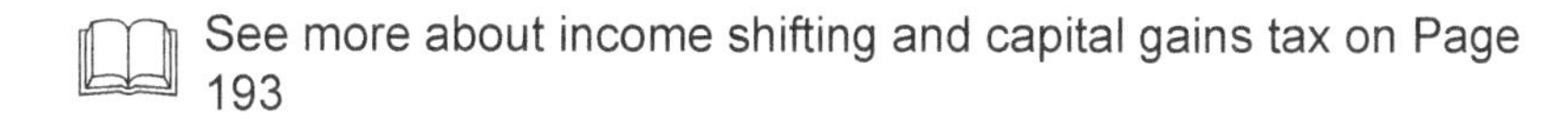
See more about income shifting and capital gains tax on Page 193

☑ Make sure you do not fall into the trap of not dividing income into personal bank accounts.

Chapter 3

Knowing Your Own Business

Chapter preview:

- Which property business do you run?
- UK property businesses explained
- What is an overseas property business?
- Understanding uncommercial lets
- Buy to sell is not investment

Most property people believe they run a single business involving letting, homes, holiday lets and buying to sell. This chapter explains why that way of thinking is completely wrong and how a property investor can run more than one property business at the same time.

Three factors define a property business:

- The status of the owner - such as a sole trader, company or business partnership

- The intended use of the property at purchase– such as doing up as a buy to sell or renting out as a buy to let or holiday let;

- The location of the property – whether the buy to let is in the UK or overseas and whether a holiday let is in the UK or European Economic Area (EEA).

  Both are separate businesses and landlords must keep separate financial records for each even though the income and expenses for both are reported on the same section of a tax return.

Here we examine ownership in more detail, while property use and location is explained in the following section.

Legal capacity is the status of the owner in relation to the ownership of the property. Legal capacities can come in many and varied forms, including:

- Sole owners
- Joint owners – including beneficial joint tenancies and tenants-in-common
- Business partnerships
- Company shareholder or director
- Trustee

Someone can own several properties in one or more of these legal capacities, and each is a separate property business that must have specific accounts and tax returns. Importantly, the profits and losses of each property business are entirely separate and may not be offset against each other.

Not only must each business keep separate financial records, but the legal capacity of the owner also determines which sections of a self-assessment tax form need completing to report income and losses.

Property tax rules separate property to let into three categories depending on use and location.

Which Property Business Do You Run?

Property investors cannot choose the category into which their property is placed nor the type of taxes they pay.

Sets of tax rules establish this.

Once a property is allocated a category, the tax rules, forms to complete and filing dates all fall into place for the investor.

The categories are:

- A UK property business - this includes buy to lets, houses in multiple occupation (HMOs) and furnished holiday lets in the UK and European Economic Area (EEA)
- An overseas property business - any letting property that does not fall into a UK property business
- Uncommercial let - a property that generates a lower than market value rent

Each category is explained in detail below, including the type of property involved, locations, tax paid and tax return forms that must be filed each year.

Before we investigate the details, you should bear in mind a property is not a part of a letting business unless a tenant is paying a commercial rent.

Examples might include a house inhabited by family or friends only paying a rent which covers the mortgage, a second home or a vacant property.

Vacant does not mean standing idle for a few weeks between lets, but one that has stood empty for some time - such as a re-furbishment project which is not yet ready for someone to live in.

Although these properties do not fall into the category of a prop-erty business, they do attract capital gains tax.

See Chapters 12-15 for more about capital gains tax

UK Property Businesses Explained

The UK encompasses England, Scotland, Wales and Northern Ireland for buy to lets, houses in multiple occupation (HMOs) and land - but holiday lets have special rules.

Qualifying properties

A buy to let or an HMO are rental homes let to tenants at a commercial rate. Generally, that means an assured shorthold tenancy is in place and the rent is paid at the going market rate.

If the property is in a void period – ie standing empty - as long as the home is marketed with a view to letting at a commercial rate, it remains part of a UK property business.

This category also includes holiday lets within the European Economic Area.

Special care should be taken when investing in holiday lets in Cyprus, although the southern two-thirds of the island are in the European Union and EEA, the northern part is a state only recognised by Turkey. Only property in the southern part of the island counts as part of a UK property business. Property in the Turkish zone would fall into an overseas property business.

European Economic Area (EEA) countries

- Austria
- Belgium
- Bulgaria
- Croatia
- Cyprus
- Czech Republic
- Denmark
- Estonia
- Finland
- France
- Germany
- Greece
- Hungary
- Iceland
- Ireland
- Italy
- Latvia
- Liechtenstein
- Lithuania
- Luxembourg
- Malta
- Netherlands
- Norway
- Poland
- Portugal
- Romania
- Slovakia
- Slovenia
- Spain
- Sweden
- United Kingdom

Furnished holiday lets

A furnished holiday let is a home let on a short term licence to guests paying a commercial rate.

Private use and letting to family or friends at a reduced rate excludes the property from being categorised as a holiday let.

To qualify as a holiday let, the home must pass all these tests:

- Be located in the UK or European Economic Area (EEA)

- Pass the availability test - be available to paying guests at a commercial rent for no less than 210 days a year
- Pass the occupancy test - be occupied by paying guests at a commercial rent for no less than 105 days a year
- Not be let for periods of 31 days or more for more than 155 days a year

The last rule allows longer lettings outside the peak holiday season, so a furnished holiday let can be rented for up to a month at a time during the holiday season and for longer periods off-season.

Applying the holiday let tests

To meet the qualifying rules, the tests must be applied as follows:

- For existing holiday lets, apply the tests for the relevant tax year or accounting period
- For new lets - for the first 12 months from the start of the first let
- When the property ceases to be a holiday let, apply the tests for the 12 months ending on the date of the last letting.

Averaging occupancy for a holiday let portfolio

Averaging rules apply to owners with two or more holiday lets. This lets owners who have a property that failed the occupancy test share excess occupancy from other homes in the portfolio, under certain circumstances:

- Each property must pass the availability test
- The occupancy test can be averaged across the portfolio, so if some are let for more than 105 days and some for fewer, the landlord can elect to adopt the average overall occupancy of the portfolio
- Averaging applies by location, so UK furnished holiday lets can be averaged or EEA furnished holiday lets can be averaged, but the two cannot be mixed.
- Averaging also comes with a time limit – the application must

be made within 12 months following January 31 after the end of the tax year that averaging is applied to

HM Revenue & Customs gives an averaging example:

Emma lets four UK holiday cottages in 2014–15 and only three qualify as furnished holiday lets according to the occupancy test - but with averaging all four qualify.

The actual letting periods are:

	Number of days let
Cottage 1	120
Cottage 2	125
Cottage 3	112
Cottage 4	64
Total	**421**

The averaging formula is:

Total days let divided by number of holiday lets

For the example, this is 421/4 =105 days

By averaging all the four properties, all the holiday lets qualify. Without averaging, cottage four would not qualify.

Period of grace election

The period of grace election allows holiday home owners to treat a year as a qualifying year if they genuinely wanted to meet the occupancy rules but failed to do.

This is only acceptable if the holiday home hit the occupancy threshold of 105 days in the year before the tax year when the period of grace is applied.

Whether the property met the occupancy rule as a standalone holiday let or due to the averaging rules does not affect matters.

If the holiday let still fails to pass the occupancy threshold in the year following the period of grace election, it can still be treated as a qualifying year.

HMRC gives an example of how to mix and match averaging and periods of grace to help a furnished holiday let meet the occupancy threshold:

Jas has three properties which he lets as furnished holiday lets. In some years property B doesn't meet the occupancy threshold.

If Jas makes elections for averaging and then for the period of grace, property B will be treated as qualifying for the period

However, if the property did not achieve the occupancy threshold after two years of grace, then the property is no longer a furnished holiday let and reverts to buy to let status.

Here's an example of how Jas could mix and match the period of grace and averaging elections to save tax:

YEAR	**1**	**2**	**3**	**4**	**5**
Cottage 1	Yes	Yes	Yes	Yes	Yes
Cottage 2	Yes	No	No	No	Yes
Cottage 3	Yes	Yes	Yes	Yes	Yes
Qualifying reason	All	Averaging	Period of grace	Period of grace	All

How to make a period of grace election

Put 'X' in Box 19 on the UK property pages section of the self-assessment tax return.

Long term holiday let occupation

Long term occupation is when someone stays in a furnished holiday let for more than 31 days.

Guests can book the holiday let for stays of more than 31 days in a row, but these days are not counted as commercial letting days.

Landlords must take care that long term rentals do not add up to more than 155 days in a year because the holiday let then becomes a buy to let and is disqualified from claiming the advantageous capital allowances and enhanced capital gains tax exemptions for the year.

If a regular guest rents the holiday property for two or more short term lets in the year and these add up to more than 31 days, then these make no difference to the property's tax status.

Sometimes unforeseen circumstances may arise, like the guest falling ill or delays affecting flights.

When this happens, a guest can stay for more than 31 days and again, the extra days make no difference to the property qualifying as a furnished holiday let.

Here's an example of long term letting where a landlord rents a furnished holiday let to four different families in the same tax year, including twice to family B:

Family	Days Let	Letting Qualifies
A	28	Yes
B	30	Yes
C	25	Yes
B	29	Yes
D	32	No
Total:	144	
Qualifying days:	**112**	

Source: HMRC

All the properties qualify as furnished holiday lets because the number of qualifying days for each adds up to more than 105 days and the long term let during the year is less than 155 days.

Part year or part property holiday lettings

If a property is only used as a furnished holiday let and is closed for part of the year, such as for refurbishment, providing the property is solely for business use and has no private use, business expenses are allowable for the complete year.

If a property is part let as holiday accommodation, business expenses and capital allowances must be apportioned pro rata between business and private use.

The same formula for apportioning rental income and business costs between owners should also be applied to capital gains tax on disposal of the property.

See Page 98 for more about splitting expenses for business and private use

Properties failing holiday let tests

A property can revert from a furnished holiday let to a buy to let if:

- It's sold
- It's turned over to private use
- The property fails the occupancy test and no averaging or period of grace election is made
- The occupancy test is failed after an averaging or a period of grace election
- One or more of the other tests are failed

Capital allowances

If the property becomes a furnished buy to let, then cessation calculations for capital allowances are made. The furniture is treated as transferred in to any other property business the owners may run.

See Chapter 9 for more about capital allowances

Completing a tax return

The financial details of a UK Property Business for income tax, including furnished holiday lets in the UK or European Economic Area (EEA) are included on the SA105 Property Pages of the Self-Assessment Tax Return for individuals and joint owners.

Capital gains tax is reported on the SA108 Capital Gains Tax Pages of the tax return.

Business partnerships complete the SA801 Partner Property Pages as well as the normal SA104 Partner Pages of the Self-Assessment Tax Return and the SA800 Partner Return.

What Is An Overseas Property Business?

Overseas for buy to let landlords comprises anywhere outside England, Scotland, Wales or Northern Ireland.

For holiday lets, overseas is anywhere outside the European Economic Area (EEA), which includes England, Scotland, Wales and Northern Ireland.

See a the list of EEA countries on Page 63

Houses in multiple occupation (HMO) are peculiar to UK law and any property outside the UK that might meet the definition is regarded as a buy to let for UK tax. Local definitions and licensing in overseas countries are ignored for UK tax, but any costs relating to licensing are allowable business expenses.

Filling in a tax return

The financial details of an overseas property business for income tax and capital gains tax are included on the SA106 Foreign Pages of the Self-Assessment Tax Return for individuals.

Business partnerships complete the SA802 Partner Foreign Pages as well as on the normal SA104 Partner Pages of the Self-Assessment Tax Return and the SA800 Partner Return.

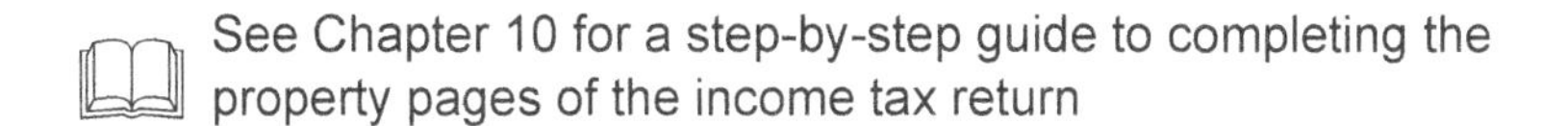
See Chapter 10 for a step-by-step guide to completing the property pages of the income tax return

Understanding Uncommercial Lets

It's common for some property investors to let friends or relatives live in a home they own for little or no rent.

For example, families buy homes for children at university or for less well-off relatives, who typically pay the running costs of the property at an amount that is normally far less than the commercial rent.

These properties are termed 'uncommercial lets' in tax law and have special rules relating to how any income or expenses are treated:

- Technically, the accounts for uncommercial lets are tax neutral as expenses may be claimed, but only up to the value of the rent received, which means they never make a profit or loss. This includes the annual 10% Wear-And-Tear allowance

See Pages 139 and 149 for more about the 10% Wear-And-Tear allowance for furnished rental properties

- Any uncommercial let losses may not be carried forward nor set off against any other property profits

House-sitting is allowed providing the property is simultaneously available for rent by a tenant at a commercial rate.

HMRC guidelines give tax inspectors the discretion to disregard a total of a month's house-sitting in any three-year period.

Beware of allowing house-sitting in a furnished holiday let as free guests staying too long might lead HMRC to disallow those days from occupancy and availability tests, which could change the property status to that of an uncommercial let.

Completing a tax return

Uncommercial lets are set apart from any other rental property and do not have to be included on any Self-Assessment Tax Return until the home is gifted or sold to someone else, when capital gains tax may be payable on any profit made from a disposal.
In tax law, property people either have an investment business

Buy To Sell Is Not Investment

that is in the UK or overseas or they are property traders running a buy to sell business.

Buy to sell is governed by different tax rules. Traders pay income tax on profits and no capital gains tax. Although counting rules for investment and property trading are conveniently the same, the way in which tax is applied to profits is completely different.

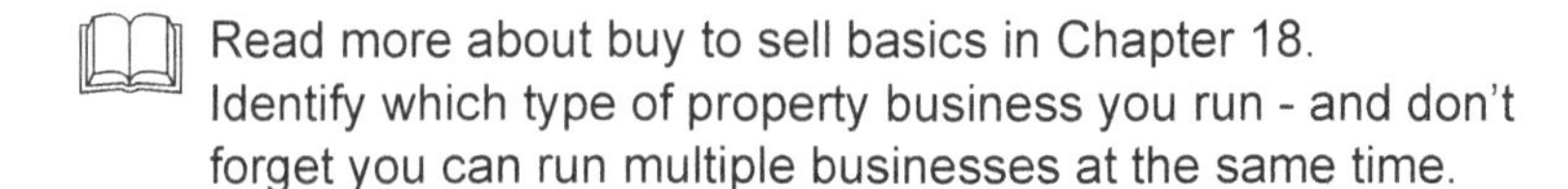

Read more about buy to sell basics in Chapter 18.
Identify which type of property business you run - and don't forget you can run multiple businesses at the same time.

Action List

- ☑ If you run holiday lets, learn about the qualifying tests and manipulate the averaging and period of grace rules to save tax.
- ☑ Don't include uncommercial lets or buy to sell properties in a UK or overseas property business.
- ☑ Keep a record of uncommercial let capital costs for your capital gains tax calculation if you dispose of the property.
- ☑ Read more about CGT in Chapters 12-15.

Part II

Managing Property Finances

Managing buy to let finances is about organising a paperwork system that suits you but delivers the business and tax information you need. Financial record keeping builds a transaction database so you can extract the detail for relevant and accurate information for your tax returns and making business decisions

Chapter 4

Keeping Good Financial Records

Chapter preview:

- When to start keeping records
- Separating property business records
- Keeping a property register
- Keeping property business accounts
- HMRC business record checks
- The Let Property Campaign

If you have to submit a tax return to HM Revenue & Customs, you only have to fill in the figures in the boxes on your tax return that relate to you and your property business. Leave all the other boxes blank.

You must keep the financial records that you used to compile those figures. HMRC can ask to see any financial documents you referred to when filling in your tax return to allow them to check you paid the correct tax.

Don't be lulled into a false sense of security, if you haven't been asked to provide evidence in the past, because they do check the information on tax returns and can demand the paperwork to back it up.

Thousands of businesses are visited by tax teams every year to check their financial records are in order. You might also receive a letter from a tax inspector querying some of your figures.

Keeping financial records is not an option – it's the law.

- If you do not keep accurate financial records or dispose of them before you should, you could end up liable for a fine

- If you do not keep accurate financial records and make a mistake in your tax return, HMRC can fine you if they believe the mistake was either careless or deliberate

- If you have a reasonable excuse for making a mistake, HMRC will not generally fine you

Reasonable excuse includes:

- Proof you keep regular and up-to-date records

- Providing evidence that you checked with HMRC or an accountancy professional if a tax issue arose that you did not understand

When talking to HMRC on the telephone, remember they exist to gather taxes, not to help you. They will record your conversation and may use the recordings to take further action against you.

Take a call reference if you do speak to HMRC on the telephone and keep a note in a diary of the date and time of the conversation, notes about the conversation and the outcome.

This counts as evidence of taking advice.

When To Start Keeping Records

It's a good idea to keep records from the day you assume ownership of a property.

Capital expenses start with the solicitor's bill and purchase price going into the property register.

Subsequently, keep records as you go rather than play catch-up at the year's end when documents are lost or you may not remember when and why you received money or paid a bill.

Try to put aside a regular couple of hours each month for book-keeping for the month before. This exercise will highlight if you have bills to pay and whether anyone owes you money.

If you've just bought or acquired your first letting property, your business does not officially start until the date of first letting, but you can still keep pre-letting expenses and put them into the accounts from the date of first letting.

To maintain accurate financial records, you must also understand a few simple book-keeping rules, which are explained in the rest of this chapter, along with information concerning the specific forms you should file.

Find out more about the date of first letting - Page 79

Separating Property Business Records

The difference between revenue and capital income and expenses is a cause of confusion for many landlords.

Revenue costs are the day-to-day expenses for running a business. Rent is revenue coming in, while the mortgage, insurance, letting agent fees and repairs are revenue going out.

You subtract revenue expenses from revenue income to give a rental profit or loss.

Capital costs are one-off expenses relating to a property, like the purchase and selling price, buying and selling costs or spending on improvements.

These are deducted from any chargeable gain when working out capital gains tax.

Find out more about capital expenses in Chapter 6

Repairs v improvements

This is the one that leads to the most mix-ups for tax professionals as well as landlords.

Repairs are like-for-like replacements. Common repairs might be replacing a part in a boiler, painting and decorating or fitting a new kitchen or bathroom.

HMRC also considers replacing old building materials with more modern ones a repair, so fitting double glazing or an uPVC door is a repair, not an improvement. The same applies to replacing old lead or copper pipes with plastic ones.

Capital expenses would be improvements to the property, such as adding a conservatory or extension.

Upgrading the fittings are also capital costs, so replacing chrome taps with gold ones is a capital cost, not a repair, while the same would apply to replacing a standard worktop with one made of granite.

To fend off queries from HMRC as to whether a cost was really revenue or capital, it's a good idea to take before and after photographs of refurbishments for filing with financial records.

The photographs will show a before and after view of each room to give an indication of what was replaced and improved.

See Chapter 6 for more about revenue and capital expenses

Keeping A Property Register

A property register is for listing the capital costs relating to a specific property so you can claim the proper amount of capital gains tax relief when you come to sell the home.

Divide the register into sections:

- Property – for details of the property, such as the address and date you assumed ownership
- Owners – a list of owners from day one and their proportion of equity. Update this section every time someone's share of equity in the property changes

Include the owner's name and address, whether they have lived in the property as their main home, the dates ownership started and ceased and their relationships with other owners.

This is important because equity transfers between spouses and civil partners are treated differently from those between other people.

- **Capital costs** – the law is very specific about which

capital expenses owners can set off against the disposal of a property. Include:

- The buying price or acquisition cost
- Any cost related to the buying, such as legal expenses and stamp duty
- Any improvement costs
- Any costs related to defending the title of the land, for example, if you called in a surveyor or lawyer to litigate a boundary or right-of-way dispute
- The selling price
- Any costs related to the sale, such as legal expenses and estate agent or auction fees

Form 17 – Keep copies and correspondence from HMRC for Form 17s in the property register.

See Page 56 for more about the Form 17

Timeline – Begin at the acquisition date, include the date of first letting and any change of use from renting to personal occupation or to a furnished holiday let. Evidence the lettings with copies of tenancy agreements.

For a furnished holiday let, keep documents showing when and where the property was advertised and for how long so you can evidence the availability test.

Start and end dates for property lets should be kept to evidence the occupation test.

The timeline should also show the date a property ceased to be a buy to let or furnished holiday let. Similarly, keep details of who lived at the property and when to prove uncommercial letting.

Date of first letting

The date of first letting of the first property is the starting date of any property business. Each business has one date of first letting, regardless of how many properties are in the portfolio.

So, a property investor with a UK property business and an overseas property business has a separate date of first letting for both.

The date of first letting is important because –

- It determines the starting date and first accounting period for the property business
- It is the date any pre-letting expenses are entered into the accounts

The date of first letting starts on the date a tenant starts paying rent.

For example, Martin buys a flat to let to tenants on November 21, 2013. The flat needs a new kitchen and bathroom plus painting and decorating before a tenant can move in.

This takes Martin a couple of months and then the property spends some time on the market before a renter signs a tenancy agreement commencing May 5, 2014. The tenant moves in on May 12, 2014.

The date of first letting is May 5, 2014 because that is the date the tenant takes over the property, regardless of whether they have moved in. Any pre-letting expenses should be entered into the accounts on May 5, 2014.

Pre-letting expenses

Buy to let properties qualify for some special tax reliefs that are often overlooked by landlords, but which can significantly reduce the amount of tax paid for many years.

Pre-letting expenses are quite straightforward, but often missed but can represent several thousands of pounds of costs if a property needs a major refurbishment before letting.

Remember, improvements are capital costs, but repairs are revenue costs and go into the accounts on the date of first letting providing they pass three tests:

- The costs were accrued no more than seven years before the date of first letting
- You have not already claimed tax relief on the expense
- The claim for the expense would have been allowed if the property business was already running

Property Business Accounts

If you run a property business as a sole or joint owner with other individuals, it's a good idea to keep simple income and expenditure records.

A spreadsheet will show if you have made a profit or loss for the year and if your records are set up properly, help you complete the right boxes on your tax return.

As an individual, you do not have to file a set of accounts with HMRC, just a summary on your tax return. If you own more than one property, keep separate accounts for each and then consolidate the figures into a profit and loss sheet for each property business you are involved in.

See Chapters 4-5 for more about keeping property accounts

Accounting periods

The first accounting period - sometimes called the basis period - for a property business is the date of first letting.

For example, if Sophie bought two properties on October 21, 2013 and intended to let one as a buy to let in Britain and the other as a furnished holiday let in Turkey.

She is starting two property businesses – a UK property business and an overseas property business.

The first renter in the UK signs a tenancy agreement on June 12, 2014 and moves in on June 20, 2014.

So, the UK property business starts on June 12, 2014 and the first basis period or accounting period starts from June 12, 2014 and runs until April 5, 2015.

The first renter in Turkey moves in on July 18, 2014, so the first basis period or accounting period for the overseas property business starts from July 18, 2014 and runs until April 5, 2015.

For the following years, the accounting periods run from April 6 until the following April 5.

Tax timetable

The main point to bear in mind is that the taxpayer has an obligation to report the income, whether HMRC asks for a tax return to be filed or not.

Officially, a landlord should tell HMRC about the new income stream by October 5 of the year following the tax year when the income was received.

This applies to the first letting property in each property business, not specific properties.

HMRC generally doesn't mind if you don't tell them as long as you file a tax return on or before January 31 of the year following the end of the tax year when rental income was first received.

This sounds confusing, but the key date is the date of first letting. In the examples above:

- Martin's date of first letting was May 5, 2014
- He should report the start of the business by October 5, 2015
- As his first accounting period is May 5, 2014 until April 5, 2015, his first tax return is due on or before January 31, 2016
- The final accounting period is from April 6 until the date letting ended for the last property in a portfolio

In Sophie's case, described earlier in this chapter, she should report the start of both of her rental businesses by October 5, 2015 and submit a tax return by January 31, 2016.

Both Martin and Sophie are due to pay any tax owed on January 31, 2016.

HMRC Business Record Checks

HM Revenue & Customs (HMRC) checks the financial record-keeping of thousands of businesses every year.

The checks began in 2012 and are designed to close a gap in the tax investigation process.

Before business record checking, HMRC had to wait for a taxpayer or company to submit a tax return and then open an inquiry if they suspected errors or wrongdoing.

This meant that taxpayers who did not submit a tax return slipped into the shadows and were able to evade proper scrutiny for a long time, if not forever.

Under the new process, HMRC looks at business records in advance regardless of whether the taxpayer files any returns.

This way, they can see if a business is keeping the right records for completing a tax return and if they are paying the right amount of tax before a return is filed.

How record checking works

HMRC will write to tell you that you are on the list for a record check, then follow up with a telephone call. The call is a screening test.

The caller will ask questions about your business and financial records and score your answers.

If you achieve the pass mark, no further action is likely. If you fail the screening test, someone from HMRC will make an appointment and come to look at your financial records.

On the visit, which lasts around two hours, HMRC will want to see your business records for the previous four months.

If you pass, the file is closed. If your record keeping is considered inadequate, HMRC can levy a range of penalties, from regular monitoring visits to fines of up to £500.

Should the inspector feel you have not paid the right amount of tax, the case is passed on to another team for further inquiries. The business record check covers income tax, capital gains tax, VAT and PAYE.

The Let Property Campaign

The Let Property Campaign is a chance for landlords who have not filed tax returns to bring their financial affairs up-to-date. Both landlords with property in the UK or overseas can take part.

The campaign is a chance for landlords to admit previous non-declaration of rental profits or property gains on which they have not paid tax. Only individual landlords letting residential property can volunteer – companies and commercial property lets are excluded.

Landlords resolving their unpaid tax issues are promised favourable terms – generally reduced interest on unpaid tax and lower penalties for failure to file tax returns. The campaign is due to end on or before April 5, 2015.

How the campaign works

Submitting the disclosure notification starts a time-limited window of opportunity: you have three months to calculate and pay any tax you owe.

Download the notification Form DO1 from the HMRC website or call the Let Property Campaign helpline on 03000 514 479 from 9am to 5pm Monday to Friday.

Read more about the Let Property Campaign on the HMRC Web site [LINK: https://www.gov.uk/let-property-campaign]

Let Property Campaign case studies

HMRC lists a number of case studies relating to landlords who have come forward under the Let Property Campaign. Checking the details will help you find out if you have undeclared property income:

> **Letting out your main home**
>
> Beena, 23, works in finance in Leeds. She bought a

two-bed flat in the city as her main home, then met a partner and moved in with him after 18 months.

She rented out her flat and the £8,400 rent coming in just covered her mortgage payments of £8,000. Beena also pays for running costs like service charges, ground rent, repairs and letting agent fees.

Around £5,000 of the mortgage is for paying interest – the rest reduces the amount borrowed, so is not allowed as a property business expense.

Beena should have reported a rental profit of £2,000 to £2,500 a year. HMRC could collect tax of less than £2,500 through her PAYE code without Beena filing a tax return.

Inheriting a holiday home

John, 53, inherited a holiday home which costs little other than monthly running costs and the odd repair.

Rather than sell, John spends some time there and rents the home out as a holiday let for a few weeks, but the lets do not pass the furnished holiday let qualifying tests for advertising and occupancy.

See Page 63 for more about furnished holiday let qualifying tests

John should file a tax return declaring his rent and expenses and pay tax on the profits. He should also split his business expenses so any private use is deducted from his claim.

See Page 109 for more about claiming property business expenses

Student let for your children

Alan and Sue have a son at university and decide to buy a flat for him to live in while away from home.

He pays no rent while mum and dad pay the mortgage and all the bills. A couple of his friends move in and pay rent to Alan and Sue. They have no rent agreement and consider the arrangement fair as their contribution towards the bills.

Alan and Sue do not declare the income on their tax returns.

Both should split the rent and expenses and file a tax return to declare any taxable profits after making adjustments to deduct their son's share of the costs.

Setting off property business losses

Rehan has had a buy to let house on an interest only mortgage for some years. The rent just covers the mortgage payments, while occasionally he has had to inject cash from his savings to cover times without a tenant.

After a few years, he realises he makes a small profit each month and is worried he owes tax. Rehan files a tax return and sets off the rolling losses from earlier years against his current profits, leaving him no tax to pay.

Rehan can only do this if he has kept accurate business records for the years in which he made a loss on his investment.

More about property business losses – Page 137

Let to buy landlords

Ketan and his wife Priya live in Sheffield, but Ketan wants to move nearer to his work in Birmingham after a promotion.

They bought their home just before the property price crash and would have to sell at a loss to move.

Instead, they buy a new home in Birmingham and let their former home, waiting for the market to improve to allow them to sell at a profit.

After three years, they still have not sold and have

rented out the property for all that time without filing any tax returns.

In that time they have accumulated a tax bill of around £3,000 and should file separate tax returns with HMRC each year to account for the rental income.

Income shifting

Paul is a higher rate taxpayer (40%), while his wife Patricia is a basic rate taxpayer (20%).

They have a buy to let property and decide to allocate 95% of the income to Patricia and 5% to Paul to reduce the tax they pay on the rental profits.

Unfortunately, they own the home as joint tenants and tax rules assume they each have a 50% share of ownership and that income and expenses should be shared equally.

However, although income shifting is an option by filing a Form 17, they did not made the arrangements at the right time, so need to recalculate their tax going back several years.

See Page 55 for more about income shifting and filing a Form 17

Action List

- ☑ Start keeping property business records from the date you acquire your first letting property.
- ☑ Set up a property register for each property, including holiday lets, second homes and uncommercial lets.
- ☑ Use the Let Property Campaign to put your tax affairs in order if they are in arrears.
- ☑ Make sure that you understand the difference between day-to-day business expenses (revenue costs) and capital expenses so you record them correctly.

Chapter 5

Property Accounts Step-by-Step

Chapter preview:

- Building a property business database
- Keeping property business accounts
- The wholly and exclusively rule
- Calculating cost centres
- Splitting income and expenses
- Paying tradesmen cash

HM revenue & Customs (HMRC) recommends backing up paper records electronically, such as saving them on a computer or storage device, like a memory stick or CD.

This applies to your property register just as much as basic financial records.

Keep a copy of the record or scans of documents safe with an online backup. Lots of services are available, including the 'Big Two' of Google Drive and Microsoft's Sky Drive.

Try free versions of Dropbox or Evernote. The advantage of them is that they are no more expensive than the Big Two, but they do not try to convert documents to another proprietary format like Google Docs or Microsoft Word or Excel.

HMRC does require taxpayers to:

- Capture the entire source document when scanning eg the front and back of each page

- Present the information on the documents in an easily readable format

Most people scan documents and save them as Adobe PDF files. If you don't have a scanner, you can use the camera on your phone, laptop or tablet to capture an image.

Divide financial records into months, keeping all the documents for April in one envelope or folder, those for May in another and so on. It is easier to search through a few documents in a folder to find something rather than going through an entire year.

Don't forget to write the month and tax year on the outside of the folder for easy reference.

When entering your records into a spreadsheet, keep a document ID column and write the number on the document in red. This will allow you to link a specific spreadsheet entry with a document.

Building A Property Business Database

Building a property business database means keeping a record of all income and expenses.

That database can then be queried by property, owner or category to give the figures needed to complete a tax return or draft accounts for a property business.

It doesn't matter if the information is captured in a written ledger, a spreadsheet or other software provided that the key data is easily accessible.

However you keep your financial records, you must still retain the primary documents to prove income and spending. Primary documents are the original copies of business paperwork, such as bank statements and invoices.

The records you should keep depend on the size and complexity of your property business and the different taxes you may have to pay.

Remember, each property business needs a separate set of accounts for revenue and capital income and expenses.

Setting up your accounting system

How to keep your accounting records is a matter of personal choice: you can use proprietary software, organise your own spreadsheet or maintain paper records.

Your decision will probably depend on the number of properties you manage.

The important point is that you should start keeping financial records from the day you buy your first investment property.

Most landlords who get into trouble with tax fail to start record keeping early enough and are forever living in fear of a call from HMRC.

Capturing the right financial information

Once you are in the habit of keeping accounts, the nitty gritty of keeping the records is quite straightforward.

There are two basic elements to record keeping; firstly entering income and expenses into a database, then querying the database to extract the business or tax information you need.

A spreadsheet or paper divided into columns will suffice for the database.

Keep a separate database for each property business.

Mark the columns like this:

> **Ref or Reference:** – This is a unique number for identifying each transaction. Write this number on the paperwork relating to the income or expense. If you need to search for the document supporting the record, it will be easier to find.
>
> **Date:** – The date income is received or the expense paid. This date is important as it determines the tax year into which the transaction falls.
>
> **Account:** – Set up a list of accounts for each separate person that either pays you or you pay and keep the information in this column

Category: – Work back from the property pages on your tax return and record each item of income and expense in the appropriate category.

The categories you will need are:

- **Rents and other income: -** Rents, rates, insurance, ground rents etc - Include service charges, council tax during voids and other similar expenses in this category.

- **Property repairs and maintenance: –** These are the day-to-day costs of maintaining a property, but capital costs are excluded.

More about revenue and capital expenses – See Page 102

- **Loan interest and other financial costs: –** This includes interest from any mortgage, overdraft or credit card plus the costs of arranging finance.

More about financial expenses – See Page 120

- **Legal, management and other professional fees: –** Put letting agent costs, any legal fees for chasing rent arrears or going to court for a possession order and accountancy fees into this category.

More about professional fees – See Page 124

- **Costs of service provided -** This category is for services you provide to tenants as a landlord, like gardening, cleaning, satellite TV or broadband. If you pay someone to do the work, their wages go in here as well.

More about providing services – See Page 125

- **Other allowable property expenses: –** Everything else is dumped under this category. The major costs that go here would be travel, home office expenses, administration running costs such as phone and broadband costs, stationery and postage.

More about property business expenses – See Chapters 6-7

- **Amount:** – The full amount of the money received or paid out in pounds and pence, including VAT if the tax is included in the transaction.

- **Notes** – A free text column where you can jot down notes about the transaction.

Every financial transaction will either be against a specific property, like rent in or a repair, or a general business expense.

Make a list of your properties and add an extra 'general' category.

Costs such as home office expenses, your phone and stationery would go under the general heading.

You should keep a worksheet for each property, with a column for each category.

At the tax year end, you can add up the values in each column to give an overall breakdown of profit or loss for each property.

For more about calculating rental profits, see Chapter 8

Extracting tax return data

Building a database of transactions for each property business is just part of the work you need to do to produce the figures for a tax return.

From your property register, you will have already identified the beneficial owners of each property with which you are an owner.

If you are the sole owner, then extracting the tax data is easy – you transfer the income and expense figures to the correct boxes on your tax return property pages and that's it.

For joint owners, there's a little maths involved, but it's not complicated. You simply take the figures for each property and split them according to the percentage share of each owner. This means splitting both the income and expenses for each owner.

See Page 132 for a worked example

Do I record income when it's due or received?

The rule of thumb is to account for income of £15,000 or more before deducting expenses or when it falls due, not when it is received.

This is called the 'accruals basis'. However, if total rents are less than £15,000 a year, you can use the 'cash basis' as income and expenses flow in and out.

The cash basis is accounting for income and expenses as they are paid, not when they are due.

Do I need an accountant?

Most landlords should easily be able to cope with keeping financial records and completing a tax return, especially with the help of this book.

If you run a property company, you must file accounts as well as personal and corporate tax returns and the record-keeping can become complicated.

Ultimately, it's down to you and how confident you feel managing the paperwork – and whether you have the time.

Keeping Property Business Accounts

Organisation is the key to keeping good financial records, so set up a process that works for you and covers the essentials.

Once you have a system, stick to it so you can manage your paperwork quickly and effectively without missing out any vital chance to make a claim to cut your tax.

Documents landlords need to keep

These are not exhaustive lists – for instance landlords with a large portfolio might employ staff, so they would need to keep payroll records.

If you run your business as a company, you may also need to keep extra records for Companies House and work to a different accounting period rather than the tax year.

Companies also pay corporation tax rather than income tax and capital gains tax, also directors may have to consider VAT if they offer a property management service.

These are the most common documents property owners should retain to track rents and expenses for income tax and capital gains tax:

Income Tax documents to keep

Document	Reason to keep
Rent statements/receipts	Proof of income
Bank and credit card statements	Record of income and payments
Paying-in slips	Proof of cash income
Tenancy agreements	Proof of occupancy
Deposit paperwork	Proof of money received that is not income
Insurance payouts	Proof of income
Receipts and invoices	Proof of payments and details of expenses
Ground rent/service charge statements	Proof of payment
Council tax statements	Proof of payment
Utility bills	Proof of payment
PAYE records	Proof of payment
Licensing documents	Proof of payment
Cheque book stubs	Proof of payment
Travel expenses/mileage records	Proof to support claim
Mortgage statements	Proof of payment
TV licence	Proof of payment
Gas and electric safety certificates	Proof of payment
Date of first letting	Sets tax timetable
Rent log	Proof of arrears/bad debts
Domestic bills	For calculating home as office claim
Business diary	Proof of hours worked/ meetings etc

Capital Gains Tax documents to keep

Document	Reason to keep
Solicitor's confirmation of price paid for property or open market valuation if gifted	CGT reducer - capital expense to set off against any chargeable gain in later years
Date of acquisition of property	Sets start of ownership
Incidental purchase costs - legal fees, stamp duty, searches, money telegraphic fees etc	CGT reducer
Conveyancing document proving type of tenancy	Shows if property is held as sole tenancy, joint tenancy or tenancy in common
Capital improvement costs	CGT reducer
Costs relating to any defence of title to the property	CGT reducer
Purchase of freehold costs	CGT reducer
Solicitor or surveyor confirmation of property value on disposal	CGT reducer
Incidental sale costs including legal fees, estate agent costs or auction fees	CGT reducer
Property register	Record of ownership for splitting CGT and claiming private residence relief (PRR)
Personal investment balance sheet	Record of cash deposit paid by buyers
Planning/building regulation documents	Supports proof of capital improvements
Documents to indicate purchase decision - such as a letting assessment	Sets tax status of property as an investment
Form 17 and declaration of trust	Proof of how property ownership is split at different stages of ownership
Probate documents for inherited property	Proof of date ownership starts

How long to keep records

Keep all the documents for at least six years after the end of the tax year to which they relate. So, documents applying to the tax year ending April 5, 2014, should be kept until April 5, 2020.

Keep them for this time even though the minimum time for keeping financial records for self-assessment tax returns is a year after the January 31 filing deadline or fifteen months after the date of sending in your tax return if you file the paperwork earlier.

Tax inquries gerneally go back six years, so playing safe and keeping records for longer is often a wise bet.

If records are lost or destroyed

If your records are lost or destroyed and you can't replace them, tell HMRC what has happened as soon as possible. You should try to recover the missing information. Ask lenders for copies of mortgage or bank statements. Be aware that they may charge for this information.

Don't delay filing a tax return while you wait for copies of records. Use what information you have available to fill in the return and amend the return later. If you can't replace the information, estimate the missing figures.

You must tell HMRC if any figures are:

- Estimates and you want HMRC to accept these as final
- Provisional and you are using them until you can confirm them with actual figures

If you provide actual figures at a later date and you've underpaid tax, you may have to pay interest and penalties.

Technically, HMRC can fine you up to £3,000 for mislaying your financial records, but in practice this rarely occurs. In these cases, the tax inspector is likely to apply 'best judgment' for any reasonable excuse.

This generally means unless you can prove expenditure, the inspector will rule you cannot set off the payment against rental profits, so you will end up paying more tax.

The Wholly And Exclusively Rule

The wholly and exclusively rule is the basic test for including income or an expense in property business accounts. HMRC measures every property business expense against this yardstick to determine whether a claim is allowed.

Three important points apply to every expense:

- A property business must only spend money for business purposes or if spent for a joint private and business purpose, split accordingly for entering in the accounts. Incidental benefit does not mean an expense is disallowed – as long as the spending is for business reasons, the whole expense is allowed.

  Take a landlord who has a holiday let in Majorca. If he went to the island to spend three months refurbishing a villa but spent some time on the beach, he could claim the trip as a business expense as relaxing in the sun was incidental to the purpose of the trip.

- If a landlord claims for a business trip and stops for a sandwich on the way, the trip expenses is not apportioned but claimed as a whole.

- If an expense is for a dual purpose – for example if a landlord takes his wife and children to an exotic location for a fortnight on the pretext that he is working for his overseas property business, then the spending is not allowed because no business purpose is measurable.

Calculating Cost Centres

Cost centres are the glue that sticks tax planning tactics together.

Landlords will never make the most of available tax reliefs and savings if income and expenses are not allocated to properties and the properties tied to owners. Income and expenses are allocated to each property to calculate the profit and loss for each owner according to their equity stake.

Setting up cost centres is easy. Each property in each property business is a separate cost centre and each business has a general cost centre for expenses that do not apply to a specific property, like telephone and office costs.

Sometimes financial transactions need splitting because of timing, private use or share of property ownership. You need some consistent formulas to apportion these costs - and should keep a note explaining the reasoning behind your thinking.

Accountants swear by accuracy, consistency and timing, which means if it's raining, wear a MAC to protect yourself from the tax man -

- Make sure income and expenses are accounted for in the correct tax year
- Apply consistent rules to splitting expenses
- Correctly enter financial figures into the accounts

After all, HMRC will fine landlords who present sloppy records, so it makes sense to have a MAC system handy.

Splitting Income And Expenses

Splitting or apportioning income and expenses ensures sure financial transactions pass the MAC test.

When to split income and expenses

Property income and expenses are split for three reasons: –

- They fail the wholly and exclusively rule because part of the spending is not for the property business.
  This would cover an expense like buying a computer that is not used exclusively as a business machine. You might calculate that the computer is used for business for 30% of the time, so the cost is split 30:70 in favour of the business
- The spending covers more than one tax year

  A typical expense here would be buildings insurance, for example, lasting from January to December. Three months of the cost falls in one tax year and the rest in the next, so the premium is divided 25:75 between the accounting periods

- The income or spending is shared among more than one cost centre, which can be a property or owner

  For instance, a profit and loss account is drawn up for the tax year for a buy to let half-owned by one person and a quarter owned each by two others, so the income and expenses are split 50:25:25 to provide each owner's figures for their tax returns

How to split income and expenses

Again, it's all about consistency, accuracy and timing – applying a consistent formula to each financial transaction to enter the correct amount in the accounts for the right tax year.

Monthly apportionment

HMRC will accept daily or monthly apportionment of revenue income and expenses.

Monthly is simpler. Just ignore April 1 to April 5 and divide by 12 and multiply by the number of months in each tax year.

For example, Emma has buildings insurance of £360 lasting from January 1, 2013 until December 31, 2013, and then renews in January 2015 for another year for £480 as she has added an extra property to her portfolio. To work out the insurance cost for the 2013-14 tax year (April 6, 2013 until April 5, 2014), do this:

- Divide £360 by 12 = £30
- April 2013 until December 2013 = 9 months x £30 = £270
- Divide £480 by 12 = £40
- January 2014 until March 2014 = 3 months x £40 = £120
- Add the two figures together to get an annual insurance total for the accounting period of £390 (£270 + £120)

Daily apportionment

This is worked out just the same as monthly apportionment, except the divisor is 365 except 12. As a rule, calculate capital expenses by daily apportionment.

Using the same example as monthly apportionment the figures are:

- Divide £360 by 365 and multiply by 275 days (April 1until December 31) = £271.23, which is rounded down to £271
- Divide £480 by 365 days and multiply by 90 days (January 1 until March 31) = £118.35, which is £118 rounded down
- Add the two figures together to get an annual insurance total for the accounting period of £389 (£271 + £118)

Percentage apportionment

If Emma had a 60% equity stake in the properties with another owner, the insurance cost would then be split again for their separate tax returns 60:40.

Emma's insurance would be 60% of the monthly apportionment – which is £390 x 60% = £234. The other owner would enter a figure of £390 x 40% on their tax return – which is £156.

Don't forget consistency – if the figures are monthly apportioned, then all owners should follow the same split method.

Paying Tradesmen Cash

Many landlords are tempted to pay cash to tradesmen to avoid VAT on an invoice.

Although the temptation may be great, the only winner is the tradesman who pocketed the cash. Cash payments are like lost records - if you cannot prove the payment you cannot claim the expense against income.

You may gain tax relief on the VAT, but if you are a high rate taxpayer paying income tax at 40% or 45%, you will miss that extra tax relief.

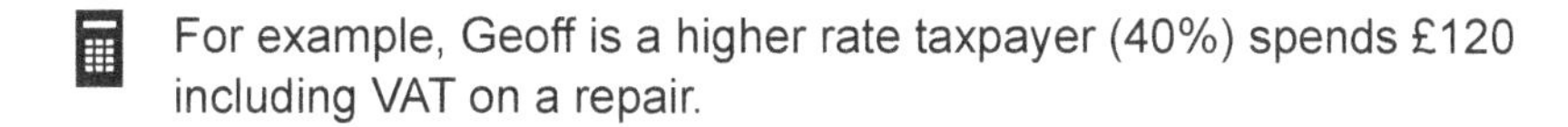

For example, Geoff is a higher rate taxpayer (40%) spends £120 including VAT on a repair.

The tradesman offers to accept £100 cash to avoid the VAT.

Because Geoff has no receipt for the cash payment, he cannot put the expense through his accounts and receives no tax offset.

If he had paid the £120 and had a receipt for the spending, he could have set off £54 – calculated as 45% of the £120 – against his rental profits or extended his rental loss to carry forward to another tax year.

Action List

☑ Set up an effective system for recording your property income and expenditure - and remember the MAC rule:

- Make sure income and expenses are accounted for in the correct tax year
- Apply consistent rules to splitting expenses
- Enter correct financial figures into the accounts accurately

☑ Separate capital and revenue income and expenses for accurate income and capital gains tax calculations.

☑ Make sure you file your financial information to support any inquiry in later years from HMRC.

☑ Understand the wholly and exclusively test and how to apply the rules to each business expense - whether capital and revenue.

☑ Devise formulas and business policies for claiming and splitting expenses according to private use, timing and shares of property ownership.

Chapter 6

Revenue v Capital Expenses

Chapter preview:

- What's the big deal about expenses?
- What is a revenue expense?
- What is a capital expense?
- Refurbishments - capital or revenue?
- Splitting repair and improvement costs

Claiming capital and revenue expenses is one of the main topics property tax accountants are asked about because the rules are so confusing.

This chapter resolves that confusion by providing a clear and concise overview of exactly what landlords can claim against tax – and which expenses fall under the revenue and capital expense categories.

Before discussing the subject, to be absolutely clear, this chapter is all about the difference between repairs and improvements to a property and how to register them into your property business accounts.

Day-to-day running costs, like travel, home office expenses and mortgage interest are all dealt with in much more detail in the chapter on landlord property business expenses.

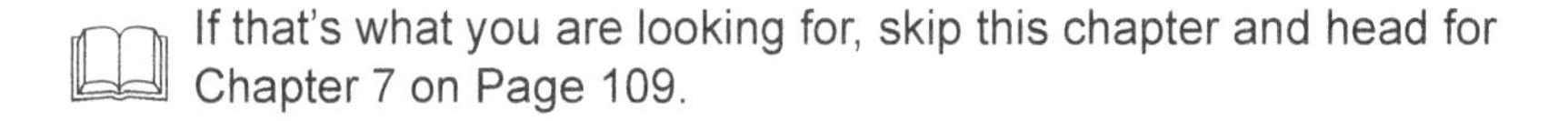

If that's what you are looking for, skip this chapter and head for Chapter 7 on Page 109.

What's The Big Deal About Expenses?

Cashflow is the main reason to make sure you separate landlord revenue and capital expenses.

Knowing the difference is crucial in determining the amount of tax relief a landlord can offset against income.

Revenue expenses are claimed in the tax year during which they arise – which means an instant return by reducing annual rental profits and the tax you pay.

That means every pound claimed in revenue expenses is subtracted from taxable profits, meaning less tax is paid.

Capital expenses are applied on disposal of a property and reduce any chargeable gain pound for pound, leading to a saving on capital gains tax.

As many landlords keep property as a permanent investment, they may never live to see a disposal and the capital expense is lost forever as the new owner cannot claim them.

What Is A Revenue Expense?

Revenue expenses are day-to-day property business spending, and in the context of this chapter that means a repair.

A repair is restoring a damaged asset to its original state by replacing a subsidiary part.

A classic example is tiles blowing off a roof during a storm.

If the tiles are simply replaced, that is a revenue expense and a repair, even if the property is re-roofed.

If the landlord takes the opportunity to improve the property by adding a loft extension at the same time, then that is classed as an improvement and goes into the capital expense category.

Common repairs

Here's a list of common repairs classed as revenue expenses:

- Exterior and interior painting and decorating
- Stone cleaning
- Damp and rot treatment
- Mending broken windows, doors, and equipment, such as cookers
- Repointing
- Replacing roof slates, flashing and gutters

What Is A Capital Expense?

Besides the list of capital costs related to buying and selling a property and defending the legal title, the Taxation of Chargeable Gains Act 1992 also says 'enhancement' or improvement costs are capital expenses.

The definition of a capital expense is adding to or upgrading the fabric of the property with something that was not there before. To qualify, it still has to be there when the property is disposed of.

Improvements often involve large expenditure, such as an extension, a loft extension or adding a conservatory or a garage, but just because the work is expensive this does not automatically make the spending a capital expense.

Capital spending can include smaller improvements, such as increasing the number of kitchen units or upgrading the worktops from woodchip to granite.

Common capital expenses

Here are some landlord expenses considered capital costs:

- Spending which adds to or improves the land or property, for example converting a barn into a holiday home
- Costs of refurbishing or repairing a property bought in a derelict or run-down state
- The cost of buying a new piece of land next to a

property that is let to increase the size of the garden or parking area

- Purchase price, acquisition costs and sale expenses of a property

Upgrading building materials and technology

A regular misconception is that replacing out-of-date building materials or technology during repairs with more modern items is a capital expense.

This is untrue – HM Revenue & Customs (HMRC) specifically allows for this type of upgrade as a revenue expense.

Examples would include:

- Replacing wooden doors and windows with uPVC equivalents
- Replacing single glazing with double glazing
- Replacing lead or copper pipes with plastic pipes

A tax inspector will agree a revenue rather than capital expense if the improvement comes with an increase in performance by exchanging old materials with new, but the replacement is a similar modern material that has taken the place of an older one – like changing imperial measure copper pipes to modern metric plastic pipes.

This is not a matter of opinion but a matter of law – the case is *Conn v Robins Brothers Ltd [1966] 43TC266*

Refurbishments - Capital Or Revenue?

Landlords and their accountants often disagree about whether the costs of refurbishing a letting property before a tenant moves in are revenue or capital costs.

The important point for a landlord is that if the refurbishment costs are treated as revenue costs, they often run into several thousands of pounds and may lead to a rental loss that precludes any tax payment for the early years of a property business.

See Page 137 for more about rolling losses to save tax

Tax law specifies identifying the 'entirety' before deciding whether a repair is an allowable business expense.

The entirety for residential accommodation is the structure of the house or a block of flats, so repairing those tiles that blow off is a revenue expense because replacing them is replacing part of the entirety that was already there.

Adding a loft extension is increasing the entirety with something that was not present before

The key points about charging refurbishment costs prior to the first tenant moving in are:

Was the property in a state to let without the refurbishment?

For example, a landlord buys a home which someone was living in that was in a reasonable state of repair but thought a fresh lick of paint would spruce the place up and make marketing easier.

If so, most tax inspectors would consider that a revenue expense – but you need to prove the work was redecorating rather than a refurbishment.

The best way to do this is with a photodiary of the home you should keep with your property register

See Page 78 for more about keeping a property register

Was the property unfit to live in and needed a major overhaul?

If the property was in a poor state of repair and needed a major refurbishment to make it habitable for tenants, the likelihood is a tax inspector will demand the expenses are categorised as capital.

HMRC goes into this in quite some detail in the online Property Income Manual (Chapter 2020) – link http://www.hmrc.gov.uk/manuals/pimmanual/pim2020.htm

HMRC gives an example in the manual: "If a fitted kitchen is refurbished the work might include the stripping out and replacing base units, wall units, the sink etc., retiling, work top replacement, repairs to floor coverings and associated plastering and rewiring.

"Provided the kitchen is replaced with a similar standard kitchen then this is a repair and the expenditure is allowable.

'If at the same time additional cabinets are fitted, increasing the storage space, or extra equipment is installed, then this element is a capital addition and not allowable - applying whatever apportionment basis is reasonable on the facts.

"If the whole kitchen is substantially upgraded, for example standard units are replaced by expensive, custom items using high quality materials, the whole expenditure will be capital."

Splitting Repair And Improvement Costs

It's easy to see that refurbishing a rental property can involve revenue and capital expenses at the same time.

The expenses are never lost, just treated in different ways for tax.

The ideal way to handle the expenses is to ask the builder for two invoices – one detailing the revenue costs and another for the capital expenses.

The revenue costs go into the annual property business accounts, while the capital costs remain on the property register until disposal of the property.

Generally, once capital costs are on the property register, the cost of maintaining the fabric of the property becomes a revenue cost.

Action List

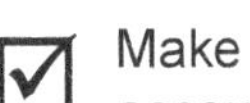

Make sure you allocate revenue expenses to property business accounts and capital expenses to your property register so the correct amount of tax is paid on each

Ask builders for detailed invoices so you can identify and apportion revenue and capital costs

Consider keeping a photodiary of repairs and improvements to a property from the day you assume ownership to dispel doubts concerning whether work carried out is a revenue or capital cost

Chapter 7

Landlord Income And Expenses

Chapter preview:

- All about property income
- Why claim business expenses?
- Putting the brakes on travel expenses
- Home as office costs
- Mortgage and financial interest
- Common landlord expenses

Solving the property business expenses conundrum for landlords and investors is not easy.

HM Revenue & Customs (HMRC) runs a topsy-turvy system for claiming business expenses that talks a lot about what can't be claimed and says very little about what can be.

HMRC has no official list of property business expenses and will not tell a landlord what they can claim on their tax returns – but will fine them for including expenses that should not be claimed.

Because this book is about empowering landlords rather than keeping them in the dark, here is a list of day-to-day revenue property business expenses all landlords should consider claiming in order to reduce their tax bills.

The list is not exhaustive, but covers most common scenarios.

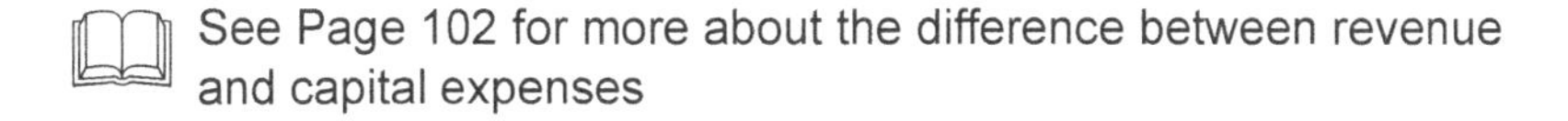

See Page 102 for more about the difference between revenue and capital expenses

All About Property Income

The first scenario to consider is one where turnover does not equal profits.

Turnover is the total income a property business generates in a tax year, and this is the figure you deduct your expenses from to arrive at a profit. You then pay tax on this figure.

To calculate turnover, add up all the money coming in from:

Rents - These can be regular or one-off payments by tenants, for example a friend renting a second home for a holiday.

If you are letting a room in your home to a lodger under Rent-A-Room, do not include this rent as turnover.

You should calculate turnover from gross rent - what the tenant pays, not the money received from the letting agent after they deduct their fees.

See Page 128 for how to calculate assessable rent

See Chapter 17 for more about Rent-A-Room

Payment in kind

If a tenant carries out some work for you, such as redecorating, and you reduce the rent, then you still record the rent that was due, not the reduced amount.

The tenant has still paid the full rent as you have received cash plus payment-in-kind to make up the full amount. Any payment in kind agreement has a cash value, and that's generally the amount the rent is reduced by.

Insurance payments

Landlords pick up two types of insurance payments - compensation for damage or loss and payments from rent guarantee policies. The first are normally set off pound for pound against repairs or the cost of new items, so the income is cancelled out by the expense making them tax neutral.

Rent guarantee payments cover bad debts never likely to be repaid, so they count as rental income.

Grants for repairs

Some local authorities and other bodies offer grants for property repairs.

Like insurance compensation, they are set off against expenses and are likely to be tax neutral.

Tenant Deposits

Tenant deposits are not your money and should be held in a tenancy deposit protection scheme.

While on deposit, they do not go through the rental accounts, and won't unless you claim some or all of the cash to cover damage, replacement locks or rent arrears.

Any retained deposit cash is treated as income in the same way as insurance pay outs and local authority grants.

Why Claim Business Expenses?

The reason for claiming property business expenses is quite simple – every pound that goes through the accounts as an expense reduces rental profits and the tax a landlord pays.

In monetary terms, that's a saving of 20p, 40p or 45p in the pound, depending on whether you are a basic, higher or top rate taxpayer.

The trick with expenses is rigorously to check every expense to make sure you claim every penny to which you are entitled.

One way of paying less tax from the same rental income is to claim every expense you can to make the taxable profit smaller.

Lots of small expenses can soon add up to a tax saving of several hundred pounds across the year.

What expenses can landlords claim?

Tax law says a landlord can reclaim any expense, providing:

- The money was spent wholly and exclusively for the property business
- The expense was a day-to-day business cost and not capital investment, like spending on buying, selling or improving a home

In this context, landlord means joint landlords and companies as well.

Categorising expenses

The SA105 UK property pages supplement for tax returns lists expenses in six categories:

- Box 24 - Rent, rates, insurance, ground rents etc
- Box 25 - Property repairs and maintenance
- Box 26 - Loan interest and other financial costs
- Box 27 - Legal, management and professional fees
- Box 28 - Costs of services provided, including wages
- Box 29 - Other allowable property expenses

Each expense list in this chapter has a number in brackets by the heading.

This number corresponds to the box number the amount should be recorded under on the tax return.

Expenses that do not fall into one of the obvious categories should be listed under Box 29, such as travel, accommodation and subsistence costs.

Putting The Brakes On Travel (29)

Claiming travel expenses all changed in the closing months of the 2013-14 tax year, when HMRC won two landmark court cases:

- Noel White v HMRC [2014] TC 03354 (Link: http://www.financeandtaxtribunals.gov.uk/judgmentfiles/j7633/TC03354.pdf)

- Dr Samadian v HMRC [2014] UKUT 0013 (TCC) (Link: http://www.tribunals.gov.uk/financeandtax/Documents/decisions/Dr-Samad-Samadian-v-HMRC.pdf

These are game changers. The results supported HMRC's argument that travel between home and a place of work is commuting and that reclaiming the costs is not allowed.

The judgments are so recent no one has had time to see how HMRC will enforce the rules. It's probable that landlord travel expenses will come under close scrutiny in tax returns submitted from January 2015.

So, here's the information landlords need to make the most of claiming property expenses:

What is travel?

Travel not only includes the cost of going from A to B, but also extra costs like tolls, hotels, meals and congestion charges.

Car, motorcycle and van owners will find claiming a set rate per mile the easiest way to keep track of travel costs.

Drivers should keep a log of business trips – noting the mileage for the first trip on or after April 6 each year. Mileage allowances are claimed per taxpayer for a tax year regardless of the vehicle the miles are travelled in.

The details to log are:

- The date of the trip
- Destination and reason for the trip

- Distance travelled
- Type of vehicle

Claiming mileage is easier than splitting the costs for business and private use of a vehicle.

The current rates per mile are:

Vehicle	First 10,000 miles	Additional mileage
Cars and vans	45p	25p
Motorcycles	24p	24p
Bicycles	20p	20p

Meals and staying overnight

Just because a landlord is away from home does not automatically allow them to claim for meals and accommodation, after all if they were at home they would not make a claim.

Reams of case law from courts and tribunals cover this area. If the trip is a legitimate property business trip, then put in a claim.

Pinning down your business base

Be aware that if a property business appoints letting agents to manage properties, the likelihood of a successful travel claim is small as they do all the administration and property visits.

Landlords who manage their own portfolios from a home office can claim travel costs from their home to a letting property and trips between properties.

If property investors have an office away from home to manage their business, trips between home and the office count as commuting and not business trips for mileage claims.

A tip here is to read the management contract signed with the agent carefully to make sure that any travel expenses claimed align with the terms of the contract.

Do not claim any travel costs that could be duplicate expenses that are already covered by the letting agent management fee.

Home Office Costs (29)

It's not unusual for landlords to run their property businesses from a home office for at least a few hours every week or to store tools and equipment in the garage.

Claiming home office expenses depends on the business use of time and space in the home.

HM Revenue & Customs (HMRC) looks closely at how home office expenses are claimed and applies a stack of rules to make sure private expenses are not attributed to a business.

New simplified accounting rules can take the sting out of calculating home office costs.

If a sole trader or business partnership turns over £81,000 or less in the year, the trader can switch to simplified accounting.

An allowance is paid for home office costs, providing the home office is used for more than 25 hours a month.

The payment takes into account household running costs, like heat, light, power, telephone and broadband costs.

For companies and other businesses outside the simplified accounting scheme, formulae are applied to calculate home office costs.

First the 'wholly and exclusively' rule is applied. This rule allows a trader to split a single bill, like electricity, between personal and business use.

The principle was established by Judge Templeman in the often quoted case of *Caillebotte v Quinn [1975] 50TC222.* The judge said: "It is possible to apportion the use and cost of a room on a time basis, and to allow the expense of the room during the hours in which it is used exclusively for business.

"In the same way as it is possible to calculate the business expenses of a car which is sometimes used for business purposes exclusively and sometimes used for pleasure."

Sometimes this is easier said than done.

The factors to be taken into account when apportioning an expense include:

> **Space:** What proportion in terms of area of the home is used for trade purposes?
>
> **Usage:** how much is consumed? This is appropriate where there is a metered or measurable supply such as electricity, gas or water.
>
> **Time:** how long is it used for trade purposes, as opposed to any other use?

Expenses broadly fall into two categories, fixed costs and running costs.

Home office fixed costs

Some home office costs relate to the whole home regardless of the time and space used for the property business.

If part of the home is set aside solely for your property business for a specific period, then you can claim these expenses based on a space and time calculation.

Here's a list of the expenses you should consider:

> **Insurance** - It's a good idea to tell your home insurer that you also work from the property.
>
> If you don't and make a claim, the insurer will try and wriggle out of a settlement because you have not disclosed relevant information that may have affected the premium.
>
> **Council tax** - If you are claiming other home fixed costs, include council tax as well.
>
> **Mortgage interest** - Divide the annual mortgage interest payment according to the time and space you use to work from home.
>
> **Rent** - Property owners cannot rent some or all of their own property back to themselves, but if they rent from another landlord, the cost can be divided

in the same way as mortgage interest for running a home office.

Repairs and maintenance - Repairs and redecoration of rooms used for business is allowed - but not for those that are not - for instance, a child's bedroom.

Don't forget any work on the outside of the home, like painting or replacing windows. Again replacing windows in rooms not used for business should be excluded.

Home office running costs

Some of the cost of running the home are variable - such as heating and lighting. That means that the more hours you work from home, the higher the bill is likely to be. If you only work a few hours, HMRC will accept a 'reasonable' claim without supporting records.

Reasonable means claiming just £2 to £6 a month.

Simplified accounting rules let landlords claim a flat rate home office allowance, providing:

- Rental income is no more than the VAT threshold for the tax year - Don't worry about accounting for VAT, the threshold is just a convenient cut-off point for simplified accounting.
- The home office is used for more than 25 hours a month

Rates for flat rate claims under simplified accounting rules are:

Business Usage A Month (hours)	Flat rate payment
25 - 50	£10
51 - 100	£18
101 plus	£26

For heavier business usage, the same time and space splitting of expenses formula is available for running costs as fixed costs.

Here is a list of some of the most common running costs claimed by a property business:

> **Cleaning** - Only cleaning costs relating to rooms used for business can be claimed if the cleaner has to cover the whole property.
>
> **Heat, light and power** - HMRC inspectors are instructed to look at the nature of the business to make sure the claim is reasonable.
>
> For example, a home-based photographer with studio lighting is likely to consume more power than a landlord with a laptop.
>
> **Telephone and mobile** - Mark off business costs on the bills and don't forget whatever percentage of calls are classed as a business expense, you can claim the same percentage of line rental.
>
> For example, if the monthly bill is £100 with rental of £20 on top, and business calls are £60, then claim 60% of the rental costs as well.
>
> **Broadband** - Calculate broadband costs in the same way as telephone and mobile costs.
>
> **Metered water charges** - Tax inspectors also monitor water bill claims.
>
> If a landlord has minor home office usage and does not have business appointments at home, it's likely any claim will be denied.

Calculating home office costs

Working out a claim for home office costs is a three step process that starts with calculating fixed and running costs of your home.

On the next page is a step-by-step calculation as a template for showing HMRC how you arrived at your claim.

Insert your own figures into a copy of the worksheet to calculate your claim. Don't forget to clip the bills that support your calculation to the worksheet.

	Fixed costs		
	Buildings insurance	£150	
	Council tax	£2,000	
	Mortgage interest	£3,500	
	Repairs	£1,500	
A	**Total:**		**£7,150**
	Running costs		
	Heat, light and power	£2,500	
	Telephone	£500	
	Broadband	£250	
	Metered water	£300	
B	**Total:**		**£3,550**
C	**Total costs (A + B)**		**£10,700**

Next comes a time and space formula that gives you a factor of how much of the home is used for a property business:

D	Number of rooms in property: (Excluding halls/kitchens/bathrooms)	6
E	Rooms used for business:	4
F	Rooms used for business as a percentage of rooms in property (E/D x 100):	66%
G	Hours a week working at home:	35
H	Time space used for business: (G/168 x 100)	21%

Lastly, apportion time and space to costs:

I	Cost apportioned to rooms used for business (CxF)	£7,062
J	Costs apportioned to time rooms used for business (IxH) - The claim for the tax return:	£1,483

Home offices and capital gains tax

Home office claims do not go hand-in-hand with any capital gains tax concerns.

The trick is not to allocate any room 100% for business, so the study can be shared as a spare bedroom with a fold-out sofa bed, or if you have children, set up as a games room as well.

Storage can be shared with bedroom wardrobes, the understairs cupboard or meetings with contractors or tenants can be held in the living room or dining room.

As long as a property investor can show the rooms are shared for non-business use, capital gains tax is not an issue.

Mortgage And Finance Interest (26)

Many landlords claim interest expenses that are too low because they relate the claim to a property rather than the source of the borrowing.

Providing borrowed money is spent on business expenses, the source of the borrowing is irrelevant.

This allows a landlord to buy property business materials on a personal overdraft or credit card while reclaiming any interest paid on the expense.

Many landlords miss out on this massive tax saving by failing to include borrowings against their own home to raise cash for buy to let deposits or refurbishments.

Only the interest is reclaimed and to gain the cash, landlords have to prove the borrowed money was spent on buying land, property or equipment for the property business or funding repairs or improvements.

Calculating mortgage interest

If you borrow against your home to raise money for your property business, you can only claim the interest on the business part of the loan.

For example, if you have a mortgage of £150,000 and borrow an extra £50,000 and spend £5,000 on a holiday and £45,000 on property, you can only claim the interest on the £45,000.

To work this out, take the total interest for the tax year (April 6 until the following April 5). You may need two mortgage statements to do this as some lenders will give annual statements running from January to December.

Say the interest for the year is £5,000, the formula is:

$$\frac{\text{Amount spent on business}}{\text{Total mortgage borrowing}} \times \text{Total mortgage interest}$$

Which works out as:

$$\frac{£45,000}{£200,000} \times £5,000 = £1,125$$

Calculating loan and finance interest

HMRC will expect to see one of two types of calculation for loan and finance interest. In this case, loan means borrowing other than a mortgage.

Whichever method you choose, stick to the calculation for the life of the loan and apply the same method to every loan. Both straight line and sum of digits are considered reasonable formulas for computing tax by HMRC.

Straight line

The formula is:

$$\frac{\text{Total loan interest paid}}{\text{Term of loan in months}} \times \text{Number of payments in tax year}$$

For a worked example, take a loan over 36 months starting in September 2013 with total interest due of £3,500 over the term. This is split into three calculations to take account of the different number of repayments in each of the tax year.

For the first tax the calculation from September to March is:

$$\frac{£3,500}{36} \times 7 = £680$$

For the next two tax years, the calculation for each year is:

$$\frac{£3{,}500}{36} \times 12 = £1{,}166$$

For the final tax year, from April to August, the calculation is:

$$\frac{£3{,}500}{36} \times 5 = £486$$

Sum of digits

This formula is more complicated and involves adding up the total of the number of months in a loan term and calculating the interest paid each month.

For example, for a 36 month loan, you add 1+2+3...+36, which comes to 666. For a £3,500 loan, with total interest of £450, the first month's interest is £450 x36/666, which equals £24. For the second month the calculation is £450 x 35/666.

This gives the annual interest paid, bearing in mind fewer payments may be made in the tax year in which the loan begins and ends..

As a check, add up the monthly repayments and the figure should equal the total interest paid on the loan.

Debit, credit and store cards (26)

Try to keep a separate card for business purchases to make calculating business interest easier and this also prevents HMRC from looking into your private finances if you are subject to a tax investigation.

Unless the card has zero starting balance, HMRC will try to turn down interest claims on these cards because of the way interest is calculated by the provider.

Other Landlord Expenses

To help slash your tax bill, here's a list of other common landlord expenses that are easy to claim and sometimes overlooked.

Mortgage fees (26)

Mortgage and finance fees are generally treated as allowable expenses - providing the property is let on a commercial basis. Mortgage costs relating to uncommercial lets are not included.

Typical costs would include payments to brokers, arrangement fees, booking fees and the like.

Repairs and improvements (25)

This rule is forever a cause of confusion for landlords. They can claim the full cost of a repair against income tax – but nothing for improvements.

Improvements are a capital cost and are held in the business until a full or part disposal of the property.

A repair is replacing or renewing part of the existing fabric of the property, like a pump for the boiler, a tile for the roof or a new kitchen. These costs are claimed against rental profits.

An improvement involves upgrading or adding something to the home – such as a garage or loft conversion. Replacing that kitchen with melamine cupboards and a chipboard worktop with one made from solid wood and granite is an improvement.

Read more about repairs and capital expenses - Page 102

Paying property business wages (28)

Landlords running buy to lets or shared letting houses cannot charge the business for their own time spent managing them.

They can however pay friends, family or employees who do not own a share of the property. For couples where each investor owns a property outright, they can pay the other to work for them.

This is also a good way to make pocket money tax deductible by paying children old enough to work an amount below the income tax and national insurance limits for odd jobs.

The rate of pay should reflect the work undertaken, so paying someone £50,000 a year to keep the books for a buy to let won't wash with HMRC.

Landlord training (29)

Setting off the costs of training courses, web site subscriptions,-books and magazines is a thorny issue. The basic rule is that training to reinforce existing skills is allowed, but spending to gain new skills is not.

For example, buying this book is reinforcing landlord skills and is an allowed expense, but going on a property investor get-rich-scheme is not, because they are teaching new skills.

Look for landlord training courses run by the Residential Landlords Association at https://www.rla.org.uk/landlord/courses/landlord_training_courses.shtml

Legal and professional costs (27)

These are bills from accountants, surveyors, lawyers and the like. Costs related to the day-to-day running of the business, such as chasing bad debts, evicting tenants in rent arrears and keeping financial records are allowed.

Costs related to buying, selling or planning applications for a property are not allowed – they go against capital gains tax on sale or gifting of the property to someone else.

Bad debts (29)

Rent arrears are the most likely bad debt for a property business.

A debt does not become 'bad' just because someone owes the money. The landlord must make some reasonable effort to recover the money, such as starting court proceedings or passing the case to a debt collector.

Once an unpaid debt slips into the bad category, the amount becomes a business expense set off against rental profits.

See Page 128 for more about bad and irrecoverable debts

Maintaining common areas (25)

Tenants share common areas in some flats – for example halls, stairs and landings.

The cost of cleaning, decorating etc for these areas are allowable expenses which can be offset in full by landlords.

Outside, looking after the garden and cleaning windows count as costs relating to common areas as well.

Landlord insurance (24)

The costs of the three main types of property business insurance are all deductible from profits. These are:

- Buildings insurance
- Landlord contents insurance
- Rent guarantee insurance

If the property is leasehold, do not claim buildings insurance - it's normally part of the service charge.

Council Tax and utilities (24)

These are allowable expenses during void periods or times when a property stands empty during redecoration or refurbishment, providing the home will be available for let when the works are finished.

Cost of services provided for tenants (28)

Any costs the tenant would normally pay but which are borne by the landlord go into this category. Common expenses would be for example, satellite or cable TV or utility bills in a shared house.

Property charges (24)

Property charges mainly come with leasehold properties, like service charges and ground rents.

Consumables (29)

Some property business costs are not property related but are often overlooked, such as:

- Printer ink

- Stationery and business cards
- Postage

Costs of properties that fail to complete

Aborted property costs when purchases fall through are considered as a cost of investment and cannot be reclaimed against income tax or capital gains tax.

Control expenses to make more profits from the same income - if you can't raise rents good money management leads to putting more cash in your pocket

Landlord's Energy Saving Allowance (35)

Landlord's Energy Saving Allowance (LESA) is a use it or lose it allowance that expires on April 5, 2015 but covers certain spending on energy saving improvements to buy to let and house in multiple occupation (HMO) properties until that date.

See Page 151 for more details about LESA

Action List

Understand the difference between capital and revenue expenses so that the right expense is offset against the right tax

Read more about capital and revenue expenses in Chapter 6

Keep workings and minutes explaining why you decided on a specific formula for a claim with the relevant financial documents to prove expenses if your figures are questioned by HMRC

See Chapter 4 for more about keeping good financial records

Chapter 8

Working Out Property Profits

Chapter preview:

- Adding up the rent
- Deducting business expenses
- Calculating 10% Wear-And-Tear
- Single owner income computation
- Multiple owner income computation
- Property business losses

This chapter looks at pulling all the information discussed in the previous chapters together to enable you to draft a set of property accounts.

We will look at drafting a set of accounts for a single landlord property business and for multiple owners with a portfolio of letting properties.

To do this, we have to draft a profit and loss account for the property business.

This chapter looks at how to put together a profit and loss account for a UK property business.

The principles are the same for letting furnished holiday lets and for an overseas property business.

Once we have put together the profit and loss account for multiple owners, we will examine how to split the figures for each owner's individual tax returns.

- Determining the income the business has received in the tax year
- Deducting any allowable expenses

This calculation will give a profit or loss for the property business.

Next, the figures need dividing according to each beneficial owner's share of the property before entering them into the approriate boxes in the SA105 property pages of a self-assessment tax return.

 This is looked at in detail on Pages 133 and 135

Adding Up The Rent

The principle to keep in mind when working out how much rent has been paid in a tax year is not how much cash has gone into the bank, but how much rent was due in the year.

So, if the tenant had paid more than the rent due in the tax year, only the amount relating to the tax year is included in the profit and loss account.

Similarly, if the tenant was in arrears, the amount due should still go into the accounts even if the full sum has not been received. Landlords need to consider the tenant's ability to pay here.

If the tenant has agreed to pay extra each month to catch up with rent arrears, then the debt is clearly not irrecoverable, but if the tenant has left the property owing a significant amount, the likelihood of recovering the rent is poor.

To write the rent off as a bad debt, HM Revenue & Customs (HMRC) generally needs some evidence that the landlord has taken steps to recover the money. In practical terms, this means proving you cannot trace a tenant,

Involving a lawyer or debt recovery agent or starting possession proceedings to evict the tenant.

Here's a worked example of how to calculate rent due in a year:

Susan owns two buy to lets that generate £500 a month rent

paid on the 6th day of each month. Both are let fully furnished on rolling tenancy agreements from January 6, 2013 onwards.

Adam rented one property and paid his rent on time each month until January 6, 2014, when he paid six month's rent in advance because he was due to work away and then take a long holiday.

Jim rented the other property. He paid his rent in full and on time until January 2014, but then stopped paying and left the property on March 5, 2014. He did not leave a forwarding address and Susan cannot find him.

She calculates her assessable rent as:

Adam	**£**	**£**
Rent received April 6, 2013 - April 5, 2014 as 12 x £500	6,000	
Rent paid in advance is carried forward to next tax year	0	
Adam's assessable rent:		**6,000**
Jim		
Rent received April 6, 2013 - January 6, 2014 as 10 x £500	5,000	
Rent due February 6, 2014 as 1 x £500	500	
Irrecoverable rent as 2 x £500	(1,000)	
Jim's assessable rent:		**4,500**
Total assessable rent		**£10,500**

Don't forget rent can include payments in kind, grants for property repairs and insurance payments.

Deducting Business Expenses

Accountants and tax inspectors talk about 'allowable business expenses' as deductions from rental income to arrive at a profit or loss for the business.

This means reviewing capital and revenue expenses and sorting them into the categories that match the tax return, then subtracting them from the assessable income earned in the year by the property business.

Going back to our landlord Susan, we have already worked out her assessable rent for the year.

Now, we need to look at her expenses and calculate her assessable income for the tax year.

	£	£
Assessable rent		10,500
Council Tax	700	
Water rates	425	
Bad debts (Irrecoverable rent)	1,000	
Insurance	300	
Central heating installation	2,000	
Depreciation of furniture	900	
Letting agent fees	650	
Repairs	450	
Total expenses		6,425
Profit		4,075

Although the statement represents a correct analysis of Susan's income and expenses for the year, she has included capital and disallowed expenses that distort her profit for tax.

The next step is to redraft the statement into a profit and loss account for her property business that only includes allowable business expenses.

To do this, we must subtract the capital expenses and transfer these to be held on her property register.

In the future, if she disposes of a property, they will be included in her capital gains tax calculation, so the capital expenses must be tagged as costs for a specific property rather than a general business expense. As the properties are furnished, we also have to consider calculating Susan's 10% Wear-And-Tear allowance.

Calculating 10% Wear-And-Tear

The 10% Wear-And-Tear Allowance is only available to landlords who rent out fully furnished buy to let homes or HMOs.

A furnished property is not defined in tax law, but means a home where a tenant can move in with their personal possessions without having to provide beds, chairs and tables etc.

Letting property is either furnished or unfurnished, there is no 'partly furnished' halfway house. If a property fails the test, the landlord cannot claim the allowance, neither can landlords renting out holiday lets or properties owned by companies.

Landlords cannot claim the purchase cost of furnishings and the allowance is available regardless of whether any furnishings are replaced in the year.

Repairs are accounted for separately.

The calculation is not 10% of the assessable rent, but 10% of net rents calculated as:

	£	£
Assessable rent		X
Less		
Irrecoverable rent	X	
Costs paid for tenants by landlord	X	
Total deductions		(X)
Net rent		X
Net rent x 10%		X

Here's the same template with Susan's figures:

	£	£
Assessable rent		10,500
Less		
Irrecoverable rent	1,000	
Costs paid for tenants by landlord	1,125	
Total deductions		(2,125)
Net rent		8,375
Net rent x 10%		837

The costs paid for tenants are Susan's Council Tax and water rates bills added together.

See Pages 146-149 for more about furnished and unfurnished properties

Single Owner Profit Computation

The key to an accurate profit income computation is keeping good financial records.

Understanding how to record income and expenses and what you are allowed to claim as a landlord makes the job of calculating profits and losses much easier.

Now we have looked at the calculations for Susan's assessable rent and 10% Wear-And-Tear allowance, we can take the figures from her list of income and expenses and confidently insert them into the profit and loss computation.

If the figure left at the end is positive, she has made a profit, and if it is negative, she has a loss.

	£	£
Assessable rent		10,500
Council Tax	700	
Water rates	425	
Bad debts (Irrecoverable rent)	1,000	
Insurance	300	
Letting agent fees	650	
Repairs	450	
Total expenses		(3,525)
10% Wear-And-Tear Allowance		(837)
Taxable profit		6,138

Now all Susan has to do is transfer the figures in her computation to the SA105 property pages on her self-assessment tax return.

See Chapter 9 for more about completing a tax return

Multiple Owners Profit Computation

Property income computations are worked out exactly the same way for properties with joint owners.

However, proportion of ownership has to be considered when completing each owner's tax return to ensure the correct figures are transposed from the computation.

If the joint owners have several properties, the computation becomes a little more complicated if they hold different proportions of shares in the properties.

In this case, work out the income computation for each property, split the figures according to share of ownership and then put together a consolidated income computation for each owner.

This consolidated computation then gives the figures for

Multiple Owner Income Computation

	Consolidated		Property 1		Property 2		Property 3	
Ownership			50%	50%	33%	66%	75%	25%
			£	£	£	£	£	£
Rental income		19,100		6,500		5,350		7.250
Less								
Mortgage interest	8.900		3,200		2,750		2,950	
Insurance	900		300		240		360	
Repairs	1,375		650		450		275	
Professional fees	1,275		400		350		525	
Total expenses		(12,450)		(4,550)		(3,790)		(4,110)
10% Wear-And-Tear		(1,910)		(650)		(535)		(725)
Assessable profit		4,740		1,300		1,025		2,415

transposing to the appropriate property pages of each owner's self-assessment tax return.

This may sound complicated, but let's work through an example. On the previous page is a consolidated income computation for a three property portfolio with two joint owners.

The owners hold different shareholdings in each property, so the next step is splitting the computation pro rata their shareholdings.

Below is the split for the first property, which is owned 50% by each owner, so we simply divide each amount in half to give the figure for each owner.

Property 1	**50% split**	
	£	£
Rental income		3,250
Less		
Mortgage interest	1,600	
Insurance	150	
Repairs	325	
Professional fees	200	
		(2,275)
10% Wear & Tear		(325)
Assessable profit		650

Now, we must do the same for each of the other properties and then put the figures together to give the consolidated property income computation for each owner.

If the three properties had a mix of owners, rather than just two with different shareholdings, follow the same rules for each property income computation and then redraft the figures.

Should one or more owners jointly own more property with other owners, follow the same rules to split and redraft the computations.

Property 2	**33% split**		**66% split**	
	£	£	£	£
Rental income		1,783		3,567
Less				
Mortgage interest	917		1,833	
Insurance	80		160	
Repairs	150		300	
Professional fees	118		232	
		(1,265)		(2,525)
10% Wear & Tear		(178)		(357)
Assessable profit		340		685

Property 3	**75% split**		**25% split**	
	£	£	£	£
Rental income		5,437		1,813
Less				
Mortgage interest	2,212		738	
Insurance	270		90	
Repairs	206		69	
Professional fees	394		131	
		(3,082)		(1,028)
10% Wear & Tear		(544)		(181)
Assessable profit		1,811		604

The final step is consolidating the split figures for each property into a consolidated income computation for each owner - and these figures then go on to the property pages of the self-assessment tax return.

Consolidated	Owner 1		Owner 2	
	£	£	£	£
Rental income		10,470		8,630
Less				
Mortgage interest	4,729		4,171	
Insurance	500		400	
Repairs	681		694	
Professional fees	712		563	
		(6,622)		(5,828)
10% Wear & Tear		(1,047)		(863)
Assessable profit		2,801		1,939

Property Business Losses

A property business makes a loss when the allowable expenses are more than the assessable rents in a tax year or other accounting period.

If one property makes a loss and others in the same property business are in profit for the year, then the loss cancels out profits pound for pound.

For example, if Brian makes a loss of £1,000 on a UK buy to let, but two other UK buy to lets make a profit of £3,500. Brian can then reduce his taxable profit to £2,500. This is calculated as £3,500 less £1,000.

A loss in a UK property business cannot be offset against profits made in a holiday letting business or overseas property business, or vice versa.

However, the rules change if:

- No other properties in the same property business have profits in the tax year

- All the properties in the property business generate a net loss

If this happens, then:

- The property business income is zero
- The loss is carried forward to offset against the first available profits in the same property business

If the next profit is less than the loss brought forward from earlier years, then take the profit away from the loss and carry the balance forward until the loss reduces to zero.

For example, Terry has several buy to lets in a UK property business.

In several years of trading he has incurred both profits and losses. Record your losses by submitting the property pages of a tax return.

See more about how to carry forward and offset losses on Page 137

Tax year		Taxable income
2011/12	Terry makes a loss of £8,300 Loss carried forward: £8,300	Nil
2012/13	Loss brought forward: £8,300 Profit: £2,400 Loss carried forward: £5,900	Nil
2013/14	Loss brought forward: £5,900 Profit: £4,800 Loss carried forward: £1,100	Nil
2014/15	Loss brought forward: £1,100 Profit: £5,100 Loss carried forward: Nil	£4,000

Action List

- ☑ Keep the workings for your calculations in case HMRC ask about how you have worked out the figures for different boxes on the property pages of the self-assessment tax return

- ☑ Don't forget to record losses to offset against future profits - there's no time limit to how long you can hold them on your books before using them

- ☑ Remember the 10% Wear-And-Tear allowance only applies to furnished buy to lets and HMOs and that the calculation is based on net, not gross rents received

Chapter 9

Cut Tax With Capital Allowances

Chapter preview:

- What are capital allowances?
- Your Annual Investment Allowance
- What is plant and machinery?
- Claiming for furniture and equipment
- 10% Wear-And-Tear Allowance explained
- Statutory Renewals Allowance

Claiming capital allowances for a property business often means working through a baffling and impenetrable thicket of rules and regulations for landlords.

In this chapter, we'll work through capital allowances rules to give you a better idea of how they can help you save tax.

Depending on the size and type of property you rent out, the savings can be considerable.

Landlords can claim capital allowances against buy to let homes, houses in multiple occupation (HMO) and furnished holiday lets.

However the rules vary between each type of property and whether they are let furnished or unfurnished.

Besides capital allowances, under some circumstances, other special reliefs for property renovation and installing equipment are also available, such as

- 10% Wear-and Tear allowance
- Statutory Renewals Allowance
- Landlord Energy Saving Allowance (LESA)

If unsure about whether to claim capital allowances or other reliefs mentioned below, talk to a professional adviser as this part of property tax comes with a lot of complicated rules.

This chapter is just an overview of the main rules rather than an exhaustive guide. Commercial property landlords can also claim a wide range of capital allowances, but these are outside the scope of this book and should be discussed with an accountant.

What Are Capital Allowances?

Capital allowances are a tax reducer like other property business expenses. They are offset against rental profits to cut the amount of income tax landlords pay.

Whereas property business expenses are day-to-day running costs, capital allowances are tax relief for one-off purchases of assets that are likely to have a life of more than a year.

The tax rule is that a business cannot offset the full cost of these items against rental income in the year that they were purchased.

Instead, a proportion of the cost is claimed annually over a number of years, and this annual percentage relief is called a capital allowance.

When to make a capital allowance claim

Capital allowances are given against plant and machinery used in a property business, but how much money and which assets the claim can be made against depends on the property use.

Landlords should allocate specific purchases to each property business, so plant and machinery capital allowances reduce the tax payable by that business.

Capital allowances go into the accounts in the tax year when the expense was incurred. If the plant and machinery is for a UK or

EEA furnished holiday let, the relief claimed is recorded on the SA105.

For an overseas property business, record them on the SA106.

 See Chapter 10 for which boxes to complete for each tax return

Your Annual Investment Allowance

Capital allowances are set off against the Annual Investment Allowance (AIA) of each property business.

The allowance changes from time to time, depending on announcements made by the Chancellor of the Exchequer in the annual Budget speech.

The AIA threshold was £250,000 from April 6, 2013 until April 5, 2014. The Chancellor than increased the amount to £500,000 until December 31, 2015. These dates are for income tax claims - companies work to different dates.

Effectively this means any capital investment in a property investment is written off against the AIA in the first year.

AIA qualifying rules

Unfortunately, claiming capital allowances under the AIA is not just a matter of totting up the value of business assets and deducting them from the tax payable.

Firstly, the expenditure has to qualify for the AIA, and then the AIA has to be adjusted depending on the length of the trading period if it is shorter or longer than 12 months.

To qualify, the expenditure must be plant or machinery:

- Purchased wholly or partly for the property business that you run
- Have an expected working life of at least two years

What you can't claim

Some assets are calculated outside the AIA, such as:

- Cars
- Plant and machinery previously used for another purpose, such as a personal computer introduced into the property business
- Plant and machinery received as a gift
- Expenditure incurred during the accounting period in which your property business stops trading

Generally, claiming capital allowances for cars is fraught with difficulties as HM Revenue & Customs (HMRC) has rules to stop owners gaining a tax advantage from private use of a vehicle.

For a property business, claiming fixed rate mileage for business travel generally gives around the same amount of tax relief a year and is much easier to prove.

If you have an extensive property portfolio and use a car just for business travel, speak to an accountant about calculating the benefits of making a capital allowances claim compared to claiming fixed rate mileage.

For more about business travel claims see Page 113

Calculating the AIA

Special rules apply to calculating the AIA if your accounting period is shorter than the tax year. AIA applies to a tax year for income tax – ie April 6 to the following April 5 – but from April 1 to March 31 for corporation tax if you have a company.

If the first year of your property business falls short of a full 12 months, then the AIA is reduced proportionately.

Example: The tax year runs for 10 months, so the AIA is reduced by 2/12.

What Is Plant And Machinery?

All property businesses except uncommercial lets can offset the cost of plant, machinery and equipment as a business cost, providing the item is not part of a residential property.

This allows landlords to claim for tools, office equipment, computers and other items used for business purposes but not exclusively in a specific property.

These items would include:

- Office furniture, including desks, chairs, filing cabinets and bookcases
- Computers, scanners, printers, phones etc
- Vans or trailers used for business purposes
- Tools – such as ladders, electric drills, lawnmowers, and vacuum cleaners etc taken from house to house etc

The cost is offset as a capital allowance against the annual investment allowance in the year the equipment is purchased. The figure is calculated separately from the rental profits and entered on the tax return in the appropriate box, depending on whether the claim is by an individual or company.

Personal use

If the equipment has any personal use, for instance a computer may be used privately as well as for business, the capital allowance is divided so only a fair and reasonable figure for business use is claimed.

This is based on the time the equipment is used. For instance, if a computer is used 20 hours a week, but the business use is 10 hours, then 50% of the cost is claimed as a capital allowance.

Calculating Capital Allowances

The formula for working out the cost of new equipment for a capital allowances claim is:

The cost of the new asset less the scrap value or sale price of item replaced

The old asset must be disposed of and not kept in reserve.

For example, a new computer costs £450 and the purchase is replacing an older computer sold on eBay for £100. The capital allowance claim is: £450 - £100 = £350

Balancing charges

Balancing charges are the reverse of tax-reducing capital allowances.

If your business disposes of an item that capital allowances have been claimed against, then the business has to repay a part of those capital allowances.

Always take the sale price or market value of the equipment even if you give it away.

That all sounds like jargon, so here's an example:

Joanna buys a lawnmower, hedge trimmer and a shredder for taking around several shared houses she owns to keep the gardens in trim.

She pays £1,800 and offsets the full amount against her AIA.

Then, she decides all that gardening is too much for her, so she hires someone to do the work.

As a result, she sells the gardening equipment for £800.

Joanna enters the £800 in Box 31 of her SA105 UK property pages or Box 20 of her SA106 foreign pages.

Timing your spending

Think about timing your capital expenses to save tax.

If you have a low amount of tax to pay in one year, but expect a higher amount in the following year, you can delay purchases that attract capital allowances.

For example, if you plan to spend money on equipment at the end of the tax year, but you owe only a small amount of tax consider putting off the expense until after the start of the next tax year to make a tax saving .

Claiming For Furniture and Equipment

Since April 2013, tax deductions for furnishings and white goods landlords provide for buy to let and shared house in multiple occupation (HMO) tenants have been restricted after an extra-statutory concession for reclaiming the costs was withdrawn by HMRC.

An extra-statutory concession is a tax relief allowed by HMRC even though the deduction is not backed by law.

Most businesses can claim capital allowances to write down the costs of investment in plant and equipment, including white goods and furnishings, but property investors cannot claim these allowances for a rented home.

However, they can claim capital allowances for equipment generally used for the property business.

Why was the concession withdrawn?

HMRC gave notice the concession was under consideration for withdrawal and asked for interested parties to submit written evidence through a consultation process.

For some reason, the consultation slipped under the radar of the major accountancy bodies and only the British Property Federation responded.

Due to the lack of response, HMRC withdrew the relief.

Since then, the Chartered Institute of Taxation (CIOT) and the Institute of Chartered Accountants of England and Wales (ICAEW) have realised the financial impact this measure has on private landlords and are gathering evidence to go back to HMRC to have the concession reinstated.

What is a furnished letting property?

To consider claiming the 10% Wear-And Tear allowance or capital allowances, landlords must first categorise their property as one of the following as different rules apply to different property businesses:

- Furnished let
- Unfurnished let
- Furnished holiday let
- Uncommercial let

A furnished let is not defined in law, but HMRC is generally considered as a rental home 'let with enough furniture, furnishings and equipment for normal residential use'. In practice, that means the home has somewhere for the tenant to sleep, sit, cook and eat.

Just supplying white goods, carpets and curtains is not enough to meet the definition, so these homes are considered unfurnished for tax purposes. In tax law, a property is either let furnished or unfurnished, terms like 'partly furnished' are ignored by tax rules.

Furnished property claims

Buy to let or shared house landlords can claim:

- Initial costs of furniture and equipment: – No claim allowed
- 10% Wear-And-Tear Allowance: – Allowed

See page 131 for how to calculate the Wear-And-Tear Allowance

- Repairs: – Allowed
- Statutory Renewals Allowance: - Claims allowed

See page 151 to read more about the Statutory Renewals Allowance

- Landlord Energy Saving Allowance (LESA): - Allowed

See page 151 for more about LESA

Don't forget these are 'either/or' reliefs and the same repair or renewal cannot be claimed more than once just because alternative reliefs are available.

Special rules for HMOs

Although landlords cannot claim capital allowances for furniture and equipment in a buy to let home, houses in multiple occupation (HMOs) are an exception.

Halls, stairs and landings are considered common areas for all tenants and do not count as the residential part of an HMO.

This allows any equipment installed in them to qualify for capital allowances.

So, landlords can claim 100% of the costs of equipment up to the AIA threshold and any amount exceeding the AIA is written-off at 18% of the cost every year.

Common communal area equipment attracting capital allowances are:

- Carpets
- Curtains
- Alarm systems
- Fire detection systems

Kitchens and bathrooms are not considered communal, so no capital allowances can't be claimed for equipment installed in them.

Unfurnished property claims

This is where taking away the extra-statutory concession has left a black hole for landlords.

For unfurnished buy to lets, landlords can claim:

- Initial costs of plant and equipment: – Not allowed
- 10% Wear-And-Tear Allowance: – Not allowed
- Repairs: – Allowed
- Statutory Renewals Allowance: - Allowed

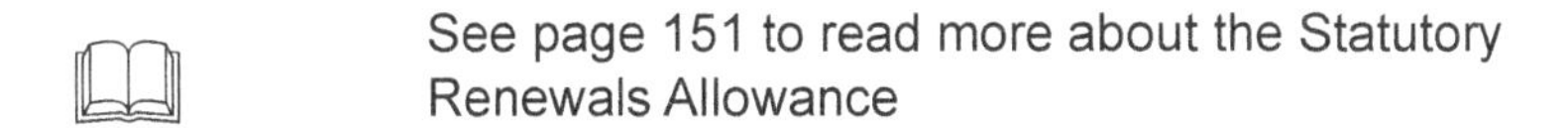
See page 151 to read more about the Statutory Renewals Allowance

- Landlords Energy Saving Allowance (LESA) - Allowed

See page 151 for more about LESA

Since April 6, 2013, landlords letting unfurnished property cannot claim the replacement cost of carpets or free-standing white goods or carpets.

Holiday let claims

Furnished holiday lets are treated as a trade rather than an investment, like buy to let or HMOs, so different rules apply to claiming for furniture, furnishings and equipment.

- Initial costs: - Initial costs of white goods, furniture, furnishings or equipment can be set off as capital allowances against the Annual Investment Allowance
- 10% Wear-And-Tear Allowance: - Not allowed
- Repairs: - Allowed
- Statutory Renewals Allowance: - Allowed

See page 151 to read more about the Statutory Renewals Allowance

- Landlord Energy Saving Allowance (LESA) - Allowed

See page 151 for more about LESA

Uncommercial lets

No claims are allowed for the initial cost, repairs or replacement of furnishings or equipment

10% Wear-And-Tear Allowance

Only landlords letting out fully furnished homes buy to lets or houses in multiple occupation (HMOs) can claim the 10% Wear-And-Tear Allowance.

Many landlords claim this as 10% of the total rents collected in their property business, but this is not the correct way to calculate the allowance.

See Chapter 8 for how to calculate Wear-And-Tear Allowance.

What does 10% Wear-And-Tear cover?

The allowance covers replacements to fixtures, fittings and equipment such as:

- Movable furniture or furnishings, such as beds or suites
- Televisions
- Fridges and freezers
- Carpets and floor-coverings
- Curtains
- Linen
- Crockery or cutlery

This list is not complete but gives an idea of the items the allowance covers.

What's not covered by 10% Wear-And-Tear

The allowance relates to furniture and fittings that make a furnished letting, but not to fixtures that are an integral part of the building.

These fixtures are those that are not moved by the tenant or owner if the property is vacated or sold, such as:

- Baths
- Washbasins
- Toilets
- Immersion heaters

- Integrated kitchen white goods – such as cookers, washers and fridges

As these items are integrated into the building, the cost of replacement is normally allowed as a repair under normal landlord day-to-day expenses.

Statutory Renewals Allowance

This allowance covers low value furniture, furnishings or equipment that have a short economic life that is likely to lead to them being regularly replaced.

These are listed on accounts as 'equipment expensed'.

Most businesses will have a policy for writing off expenses under the Statutory Renewals Allowance.

For example, capital expenditure of £150 or less would go into this section, but watch that the expense only covers the replacement, not the initial purchase of any items.

Claims would be for items like mobile phones, software, tools, lawnmowers, vacuum cleaners and office furniture and equipment.

HMRC specifies that this allowance should not cover freestanding white goods or carpets.

Landlord Energy Saving Allowance

The Landlord Energy Saving Allowance (LESA) can reduce tax bills by up to £1,500 a property a year in your portfolio.

If a property is jointly owned the allowance is still capped at £1,500 a property.

Joint owners can make a claim by either:

- Splitting the LESA claim according to the percentage of the property each owns, such as a home owned 75:25 with a £1,500 claim would be split £1,125 for one owner and £375 for the other

Or

- According to the money each spends on the improvements, for example, if one owner spends £1,000 and the other £500, then they would each claim the amount they personally spent.

LESA is not a capital allowance, but a relief against rental profits in the year claimed by inserting the total of qualifying spending in Box 35 of your SA105 property pages.

Overseas landlords complete Box 22 of the SA106 foreign pages, providing tax is paid on overseas property rental profits in the UK - and it's not a holiday let.

LESA caims stop on April 5, 2015 unless the allowance is renewed in Budget 2015.

What you can claim

You can claim LESA against the costs of buying and installing energy-saving products for rental properties.

These include:

- Cavity or solid wall insulation
- Loft insulation
- Draught-proofing
- Insulating hot water systems
- Floor insulation

What you can't claim

You can't claim LESA if:

- You are claiming Rent-A-Room relief
- The home is rented as a furnished holiday let
- You install the energy-saving items yourself – in this

case you can claim the purchase cost under LESA but nothing for installing them

- The cost is a pre-letting expense spent more than six months before the date of first letting

See more about pre-letting expenses on Page 80

Action List

☑ Make sure you are saving the most possible tax by claiming the most you can from capital allowances, 10% Wear-And-Tear Allowance, Statutory Renewals Allowances and the Landlord's Energy Saving Allowance.

☑ Read the dates, financial limits, terms and conditions for making claims carefully as they often change in the annual Budget

☑ Consider installing integrated white goods when you replace a kitchen in an unfurnished rental home. This makes replacing a fridge or washing machine a repair, not a replacement.

Chapter 10

Filling In Property Tax Returns

Chapter preview:

- Filling in the SA105 UK property pages
- Furnished holiday lets in the UK or EEA
- Filling in the SA106 overseas property pages
- Foreign Tax Credit Relief Explained

Because we 'reverse engineered' our transaction database from the SA105 property pages of the tax return, all we are left to do after splitting the figures between owners is to transfer them to the appropriate boxes on the return.

The SA105 supplement is for reporting landlord rental profits and losses. Capital gains are dealt with on the SA108 supplement and no capital expenses should be included on the SA105.

The SA105 property pages change slightly from year to year in line with Budget announcements from the Chancellor of the Exchequer and changes in tax law. Here, we are following the 2013-14 tax return.

The SA106 foreign pages are completed for an overseas property business and follow a similar but simplified format to the SA105 property pages.

In this chapter, you will go step-by-step through completing the SA105 and SA106 property pages of the self-assessment tax return for the 2013-14 tax year. You can download copies from the HM Revenue & Customs (HMRC) web site.

The SA105 UK property return is at http://www.hmrc.gov.uk/forms/sa105.pdf and the SA106 foreign pages are at http://www.hmrc.gov.uk/forms/sa106.pdf

The property pages are divided into several sections in line with the main headings below. Don't forget the tax return is individual to you, so ensure the amounts you enter follow the proportions you own of each property.

Filling In The SA105 UK Property Pages

Your name - Your full name

Your Unique Taxpayer Reference (UTR) – This is a 10-digit number sent by HMRC. You cannot submit a tax return online without a UTR.

Applying for a Unique Taxpayer Reference

To file a tax return online you need an HMRC online account to access the Government Gateway.

To open an account sign up through HMRC's online services – https://www.gov.uk/how-to-send-self-assessment-online/sign-up-for-an-online-account

Expect to wait seven working days to set up your online account as HMRC will post you an activation code so you can access your account.

If you file from overseas, this can take up to 21 days to arrive.

UK Property Details

Box 1 - Number of properties rented out – Include all buy to lets, houses in multiple occupation (HMO) and furnished holiday lets that are part of this business, whether you are a sole or joint owner. Do not include uncommercial lets.

See Page 69 for a definition of an uncommercial let

Box 2 - If property income ceased – Put an 'X' in the box if you do not expect to receive any UK property income in the next tax year

Box 3 - Jointly let property – If you share ownership of any property, put an 'X' in this box

Box 4 - Rent-A-Room Relief – If you are claiming Rent-A-Room relief of £4,250 or less, put an 'X' in this box.

If Rent-A-Room is your only rental income, the job is done and you do not have to go any further down the page.

Furnished Holiday Lets In The UK Or EEA

Do not forget to keep separate business records for any UK furnished holiday lets and those in the European Economic Area (EEA).

The tax information for both businesses is reported on the same first page of the SA105, but with a page for each business.

Leave Boxes 5 to 19 blank if you do not have any UK or EEA holiday lets. Here's a box-by-box guide of the information you should provide:

Box 5 - Income - This is the total of all rents due and any payments for other holiday let services you have sold to tenants during the year

Box 6 - Rent paid, repairs, insurance and cost of services provided - If you sublet the holiday let, the rent you pay goes in this box together with the total you have paid in the year for repairs and insurance.

Cost of services provided means services you have paid for on behalf of the tenants, such as satellite TV.

Box 7 - Loan interest and other financial costs – Mortgage and other credit interest payments go here.

Box 8 - Legal, management and other professional fees – These relate to day-to-day costs, such as accountant and letting agent fees, and lawyer's costs chasing unpaid rents. Capital costs for buying and selling property go to the property register.

Box 9 - Other allowable property expenses – This is a default box for general property expenses, such as travel, home office, consumables and anything else that does not come under one of the other headings.

Box 10 - Private Use Adjustment – Any deductions for the owner's private use of the property. In practice, this is left blank and costs are apportioned when entered in your accounts.

Box 11 - Balancing charges – Adjustments for selling assets for which capital allowances have been claimed.

See Page 145 for more information about balancing charges

Box 12 - Capital allowances – Tax reducers on equipment bought for the business, such as computers, office furniture, tools and vehicles

See Chapter 9 for more about capital allowances

Box 13 - Adjusted profit – This calculation takes the rental income and deducts any adjustments for private use or balancing charges.

The formula is:

Income – (Private Use Adjustment + Balancing charges)

This is calculated as Box 5 – (Box 10 + Box 11)

Box 14 - Loss brought forward against this year's profits –

- If you only have a holiday letting business, put any loss accumulated in previous tax years up to the amount of profit this year here
- If you have other UK letting property and no losses other than holiday lets, put any loss accumulated in previous tax years up to the amount of profit this year here, but remember to deduct the amount from any figure you might put in Box 39

Box 15 - Taxable profit for the year – This is the adjusted profit less any losses brought forward, ie Box 13 – Box 14. If you have made a loss leave this box blank.

Box 16 - Loss for the year – Add the amounts in Boxes 6 to 9 inclusive plus Box 12, then subtract the amounts in Box 5 + Box 10 + Box 11.

The worksheet below gives a step-by-step pro forma calculation.

Worksheet for holiday letting profits

A Income (Box 5)		£X
B Private use adjustment (Box 10)		£X
C Balancing charges (Box 11)		£X
D Total income (Add Boxes A to C):		**£X**
Less		
E Expenses (Box 6)	£X	
F Loan interest (Box 7)	£X	
G Professional fees (Box 8)	£X	
H Other expenses (Box 9)	£X	
I Capital allowances (Box 12)	£X	
J Total expenses (Add Boxes E to I):		**£X**
K Profit or loss (Box D - Box J):		**£X**

If Box K is zero or more, transfer the amount to Box 13 on your tax return. If Box K is negative, transfer the amount to Box 16.

Box 17 - Total loss to carry forward – If you have brought forward a holiday let loss, add this to the amount in Box 16 and carry them forward until the next tax year.

Box 18 - To differentiate the EEA holiday letting business, put an

'X' in Box 18, but leave this blank for any UK holiday lets.

See Page 63 for a list of EEA countries.

Box 19 - To make a period of grace election, mark this box 'X'.

See Page 65 for more about period of grace elections

UK Property Business

This page of the SA105 property pages is about calculating tax for a UK property business, excluding holiday lets.

Do not include any amounts already entered under holiday lets as they will become duplicate entries and give a false profit or loss figure for tax.

Property income

Box 20 - Total rents and other income - This is the total of any income you have earned from letting property, including insurance pay outs, payments in kind or grants for repairs.

Box 21 - Tax already paid on income listed in Box 20, - Such as if you are a non-resident landlord and have had income deducted at source by a letting agent.

See more about non-resident landlords in Chapter 19

Box 22 - Premiums for grant of a lease – To calculate the value of a lease, complete the form below and enter the figure from Box E on the worksheet into this box.

Worksheet for premiums for grant of a lease

A	Premium	£X
B	Number of complete periods of 12 months in the lease ignoring the first 12 months	X
C	50 less Box B	X
D	Box C divided by 50	X
E	Box A multiplied by Box D	£X

Box 23 - Reverse premiums and inducements – Leave this box empty unless you were paid an inducement or incentive to let a property other than your main home

Property expenses

To make this section easier, refer back to Chapter 7's list of landlord expenses on Page 109.

Each expense is listed with a number from 24 to 29 as a guide to which box should include the amount on your tax return.

Box 24 - Rent, rates, insurance, ground rents – Include rent you pay for a property you rent to someone else, council tax, water rates and service charges.

Box 25 - Property repairs and maintenance – General running costs, but do not enter any capital costs as these should be held on your property register.

Box 26 - Loan interest and other financial costs – Besides mortgage and other credit interest, this box should also include a mortgage broker or IFA's costs for arranging a loan.

Box 27 - Legal, management and other professional fees – Add together charges from lawyers to possess a property or chase rent arrears, letting agent costs, and accountancy fees. Include the cost of completing your personal tax return, which is allowed as a concession by HMRC.

Box 28 - Costs of services provided, including wages – These costs cover any services paid by the landlord, such as cleaning, gardening, cable TV and utility bills in an HMO. Also any wages you pay direct employees, but not any payments to property owners for their time, as this is not allowable.

Box 29 - Other allowable property expenses – This is the default for travel, home office and general property business costs which don't fit the other categories, such as telephone, postage and printer consumables.

Calculating your taxable profit or loss

Working out whether you have made a profit or loss is simply a matter of adding up any income and deducting any expenses to leave a net or adjusted figure. If the amount is positive, you have made a profit, but if it is negative, you have a loss.

Before you enter figures in the computation form, you must source a few more numbers:

Box 30 - Private use adjustment – This is for subtracting any personal costs you have incurred from living in a letting property as your home.

Box 31 - Balancing charges – Adjustments for selling assets for which capital allowances have been claimed.

See Page 145 for more information about balancing charges

Box 32 - Annual Investment Allowance (AIA) – For this tax year and until January 1, 2015, the AIA is £250,000. The allowance is offset against equipment and machinery used in a property business.

Capital allowances cannot be set off against equipment or machinery installed in residential property.

See more about the Annual Investment Allowance on Page 142

Box 33 - Business Premises Renovation Allowance (BPRA) – For commercial property investors who bring a disused business building back into use

See more about BPRA on page 161

Box 34 - Other capital allowances – Generally for bigger businesses writing down assets over time

See more about other capital allowances – Page 140

Box 35 - Landlord Energy Saving Allowance – This box is for spending on energy saving measures for residential property, excluding any Rent-A-Room lettings.

See more about LESA – Page 151

Box 36 - 10% Wear and Tear Allowance – This is for fully furnished lets excluding holiday lets and any Rent-A-Room lettings. The allowance is calculated as:

(Total rents received – (Irrecoverable rent arrears + costs paid by the landlord on behalf of tenants)) x 10%

Costs paid by the landlord would include spending such as Council Tax or utility bills that should fall to the tenants.

See Page 149 for more about the10% Wear-And-Tear Allowance

Box 37 - Rent-A-Room exempt amount – If any Rent-A-Room income is included in Box 20, enter the figure here up to £4,250 if you let the property on your own or up to £2,125 if you are a joint owner.

See Page 250 for more about Rent-A-Room tax relief

Box 38 - Adjusted profit for the tax year – Insert the figure from Box O after completing the worksheet on the next page.

Box 39 - Loss brought forward – This figure comes from last year's tax return if your property business is bringing a rental loss over from previous tax years.

Box 40 - Taxable profit – This is the rental profit on which you pay income tax. Subtract Box 39 from Box 38 for the final figure.

If the amount in Box 39 is larger than that in Box 38, leave Box 40 blank.

Box 41 - Adjusted loss for year – If you have left Box 40 blank because Box O on the worksheet is negative, enter the amount here unless you have furnished holiday let profits.

If you have furnished holiday let profits, complete Boxes P and Q on the worksheet and enter the figure in Box P.

Box 42 - Loss set off against other income in the tax year – Leave blank unless you have specific agricultural expenses or balancing charges that exceed capital allowances.

Box 43 - Losses to carry forward – Enter any unused losses brought forward from previous years plus any additional loss (Box 41) from this year. This figure will go into Box 39 on next year's SA105.

UK property business profit worksheet

A	Total rents (Box 20)	£X	
B	Lease premiums (Box 22)	£X	
C	Reverse premiums (Box 23)	£X	
D	Private use adjustment (Box 30)	£X	
E	Balancing charges (Box 31)	£X	
F	**(Add A to E)**		**£X**
	Less		
G	Expenses (Boxes 24 to 29)	£X	
H	Capital allowances (Box 32 + Box 34)	£X	
I	Business Premises Renovation Allowance (Box 33)	£X	
J	Landlord Energy Saving Allowance (Box 35)	£X	
K	10% Wear-And-Tear Allowance (Box 36)	£X	
L	Rent-A-Room exemption (Box 37)	£X	
M	**(Add G to L)**		**£X**
O	**Adjusted profit or loss (F - M)**		**£X**

Profits in Box O go to Box 38 of the SA105, losses to Box 41.

If you have a rental loss but furnished holiday let profits, enter the holiday profits up to the value of Box O in Box P.

You can also use any holiday losses brought forward from earlier years in Box 39 of your tax return against any balance of holiday let profits.

P	Loss deducted from holiday let profits	**£X**
Q	Reduced loss (Box O - Box P)	**£X**

Filling In The SA106 Overseas Tax Return

The SA106 foreign property pages apply to rental income and expenses for any overseas buy to lets outside the UK or furnished holiday lets outside the European Economic Area.

Unlike UK or EEA holiday lets, overseas holiday lets are treated for tax in the same way as buy to lets, eliminating the need to keep separate accounts.

UK taxpayers must declare all overseas rental income regardless of whether the income is brought into the UK or not, unless they are taxed on the remittance basis.

Like a SA105, a taxpayer cannot submit a SA106 online without filling in their full name or a Unique Taxpayer Reference (UTR).

For information about acquiring a UTR, see Page 155 earlier in this chapter.

Overseas Property Income And Expenses

The property income and expenses section starts on Page 4 of the SA106 foreign pages.

Only complete Boxes 14 to 24 if:

- You have a singles overseas rental property

  Or

- You have more than one property in the same country and the income is remittable to the UK

  Or

- You have more than one property in the same country and the income is remittable to the UK but no foreign tax has been deducted

If you have two or more overseas properties in different countries and have paid some tax abroad on the rental income, complete SA106 pages F4 and F5 Boxes 14 to 24 for each property.

Include separate F4 and F5 pages for each property. Also fill in columns A to F and Boxes 25 to 32.

Box 14 - Total rents - This section includes all overseas property income, leaving out any taxable premiums for granting a lease.

Box 15 - Number of overseas properties - All the properties that are part of your overseas property business, excluding any uncommercial lets.

See Page 69 for a definition of an uncommercial let

Box 16 - Premiums paid for the grant of a lease - Calculate the figure from the worksheet on Page 159 earlier in this chapter.

Box 17 - Property business expenses - This box includes all property expenses that are broken down into Boxes 25 to 29 of the SA105 property pages.

These are listed in Chapter 7

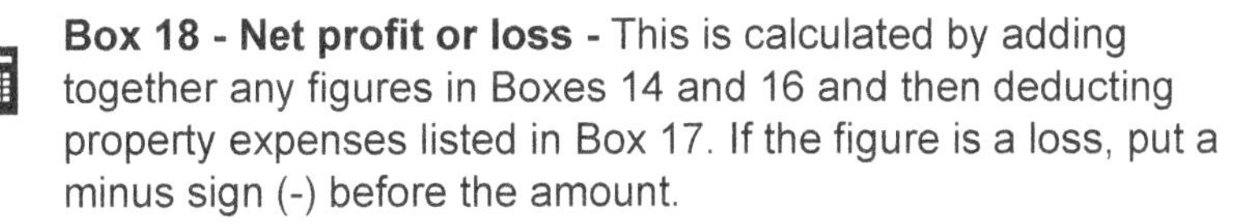
Box 18 - Net profit or loss - This is calculated by adding together any figures in Boxes 14 and 16 and then deducting property expenses listed in Box 17. If the figure is a loss, put a minus sign (-) before the amount.

Box 19 - Private use adjustment - Apportion any costs relating to private use of the property here. For example, if you stay at the property for three months of the year and rent to paying guests for the rest of the time, then work out 3/12 of the expenses and put the amount in this box.

Box 20 - Balancing charges - These are the proceeds from disposing of business assets for which you have claimed capital allowances.

See more about balancing charges on Page 145

Box 21 - Capital allowances - Capital allowances are tax relief claimed against investing in assets for a business. In some cases, landlords can claim them for an overseas property business.

See more about other capital allowances on Page 140

Box 22 Landlord Energy Saving Allowance (LESA) - This box is for any qualifying energy saving measures

See Page 151 for more about LESA

Box 23 - 10% Wear-And-Tear Allowance - Tax relief for letting fully furnished homes.

See Pages 131 and 149 for more about the 10% Wear-And-Tear Allowance

Box 24 - Adjusted profit or loss - The amount is calculated by adding the figures in Boxes 18 to 20, and then subtracting the amounts in Boxes 21,22 and 23.

Completing the country summaries

If you have filled in Boxes 14 to 24 on the SA106, you have to summarise the figures by country.

This is because each country is a separate tax jurisdiction and HM Revenue & Customs want to see how much tax, if any, you have paid in each.

Completing this section correctly also avoids double taxation on rental profits.

Each country has a three letter code which must be entered on the summary.

If you have properties in more countries than the five slots on the return, then duplicate the pages to give more space and pin them together.

The summary is divided into columns and boxes for bringing forward losses to adjust the profits.

Column A - Country code - Enter the country code.

Column B - Adjusted profit or loss - Take the total for all properties in that country by adding together Box 24 for each.

Column C - Foreign tax paid - Enter the amount of any tax you have paid to an overseas tax authority in respect of the profits in Box 24 or any tax withheld by a letting agent.

Column D - UK Tax - Enter any tax you have already paid in the UK in respect of the adjusted profit ion Box 24.

Column E - Foreign Tax Credit Relief - If you are claiming Foreign Tax Credit Relief, put an 'X' in the box.

See more about Foreign Tax Credit Relief later on the next page.

Column F - Taxable amount - If claiming Foreign Tax Credit Relief and you have a profit in Column B, copy that figure in this box.

If you have one overseas property or net losses from any overseas property, leave this box blank.

If you have two or more overseas properties in the same country and a mix of rental profits and losses, deduct the total losses from the total profits.

If you are not claiming Foreign Tax Credit Relief, the figure for this box is whatever is in Column B less any amount in Column C.

Box 25 - Total adjusted profit or loss - Add up any profits and subtract any losses entered in Column B to give the total adjusted profit or loss for your overseas property business.

Box 26 - Loss brought forward - Enter the figure from Box 32 on your last year's SA106 here. If the figure is zero, leave blank.

Box 27 - Total taxable profits - Subtract Box 26 from Box 25 and enter the figure if it is more than zero. If not, leave blank.

Box 28 - Total foreign tax - This the total of any amounts in Column C.

Box 29 - Total UK tax paid - This is the total of Column D.

Box 30 - Total taxable amount - The total of Column F.

Box 31 - Loss offset against total income - This is a limited claim only allowable if the amount in Box 21 is more than that in Box 20. If so, the loss is restricted to the lowest of:

- Box 21 minus Box 20

- The loss in Box 24
- Either £50,000 or 25% of any other income, whichever is the greatest

Box 32 - Loss to carry forward - Any unused property losses to carry forward to offset against future overseas property profits.

Foreign Tax Credit Relief Explained

Depending on where your overseas properties are located, you may have to pay income tax locally on your rental profits.

Britain has double taxation agreements in place with many countries so UK resident landlords can avoid paying income tax on the same rental profits twice - once to the local tax authority and again in the UK.

The situation varies between countries. For instance Dubai has no income tax, but landlords with rental homes in the United States will pay tax to the Internal Revenue Service.

If the foreign tax is more than the UK tax, you can offset the tax you would have paid in the UK, but HMRC will not pay you a credit for the excess amount paid overseas.

This is termed Foreign Tax Credit Relief.

A point to watch is that expenses you may claim overseas are sometimes different to those you can claim in the UK, so some landlords can have a tax profit in one country and a tax loss in another on the same property.

An additional complication is many countries operate a different tax year to the UK and will withhold tax from rents.

This means factoring in extra costs for employing a local accountant as well as one in the UK, as UK accountants are rarely qualified or experienced enough to give cross-border tax advice.

Claiming tax credits against overseas profits

Opting for Foreign Tax Credit Relief is generally the best way to pay the lowest amount of income tax on overseas property business profits.

Landlords can either claim the relief or deduct the foreign tax paid from the taxable amount.

Whichever method is adopted, you cannot switch from one to the other, you must continue with the method for all overseas properties and across future years.

For example, Martin has overseas rental profits of £5,000 and had £750 tax withheld. He is a basic rate taxpayer, so pays income tax at 20%.

If he claims Foreign Tax Credit Relief, his tax liability in the UK would be £5,000 x 20%, which is £1,000.

This makes his tax due £1,000 less £750, which is £250. This makes his total liability £1,000.

If he deducted the foreign tax, the calculation changes. His UK taxable profit is £5,000 less £750, which is £4,250.

His basic rate income tax becomes £4,250 x 20%, which is £850. His total income tax liability is then £1,600.

Foreign Tax Credit Relief restrictions

Not every landlord can claim the relief - the restrictions are:

- The landlord must be tax resident in the UK.
- The income must be paid from overseas and taxable under the laws of the country where it arises.
- The relief cannot be more than the UK tax on the same income.
- If the UK has a double taxation agreement with the country where the income arises, relief is restricted to the minimum local tax payable under the agreement.

Action List

☑ Take time to understand the figures you need to put on your tax returns and work backwards to configure the way you keep you property business accounts

☑ Allocating income and expenses to cost centres in line with the boxes makes book-keeping a lot easier as your accounts will automatically slot into the right place on the returns

☑ Use the worksheets to calculate profits and losses and file them to show how you arrive at the amounts you enter on your tax returns if HMRC ask for your workings

If you are an overseas landlord, watch out for tax traps such as forgetting to rework overseas tax returns against the UK tax year

☑ Run the numbers on claiming Foreign Tax Credit Relief against deducting tax paid overseas to see which method works best for you

Chapter 11

Property Tax Return Checklist

Chapter preview:

- Income and expenses tax traps
- Watching your personal spending
- Accounting for capital costs
- Checking capital allowances

To reduce errors in tax returns, HM Revenue & Customs (HMRC) has devised a series of tax toolkits for professional advisers.

Several of the toolkits cover property tax. They are designed to highlight the figures on tax returns where tax inspectors look to catch landlords avoiding tax.

Logically, if you run through the tax toolkit every time you submit a tax return and cover these points, you should be less likely to fall foul of an investigation.

This chapter looks at the tax toolkits for property people and condenses the main points for landlord tax returns.

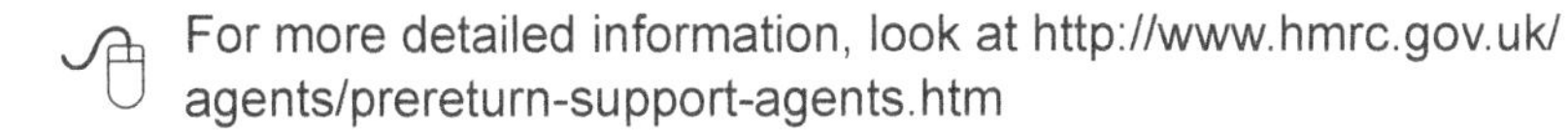

For more detailed information, look at http://www.hmrc.gov.uk/agents/prereturn-support-agents.htm

The link includes a video on how to use the toolkits and links to download full versions of each checklist.

In the text below, you can follow links to read more in this book about the specific checklist points. The link to the full checklist is at the end of each section.

Four toolkits relate to the SA 105 Property Pages and SA106 Foreign Pages.

Income And Expenses Tax Traps

1. Include all money or payments in kind received as rents.

   Watch out for net receipts, such as letting agent payments that may have had deductions before payment. The correct figure for the accounts is the gross figure, which is the payment received before any deductions.

   See Chapter 7 – All About Property Income on Page 110

2. Has the right tax treatment been applied to tenant deposits?

   If part of a deposit has been retained for repairs, payment of rent arrears or changing locks, then this money goes into the accounts as income and the appropriate deductions are entered as expenses.

   Deposits subject to tenancy deposit protection rules do not go through the business books unless an amount is retained at the end of the tenancy.

3. If a property is jointly owned, have the income and expenses been divided pro rata ownership shares?

   These amounts will be split 50:50 if the joint owners are spouses unless a Form 17 has been filed.

   See Chapter 2 – Income Shifting Explained on Page 55

4. If a property is overseas, has this been identified and the accounting records kept separate from any UK property business?

See Chapter 3 – Which Property Businesses Do You run on Page 60

5. If any furnished holiday lets are identified in the UK or EEA, have all the qualifying conditions been met?

   HM Revenue & Customs (HMRC) will check:

   Whether the property is

   - In the UK, European Economic Area (EEA) or elsewhere
   - Furnished
   - Let on a commercial basis to make a profit
   - That all qualifying conditions are met

See Chapter 3 – UK Property Businesses Explained on Page 62

6. Have expenses gone through a review to separate capital from revenue costs and have repairs to newly acquired property been treated properly?

   If the property was in a run-down state and not fit to rent out, then the repairs are likely to be capital costs, while if the home was habitable and has just been cleaned up, they are revenue expenses.

See Chapter 6 – Revenue v Capital Expenses on Page 102

7. Have legal, professional and other fees incurred in acquiring property been allocated appropriately?

   Fees relating to acquiring the asset, like stamp duty and legal costs are capital expenses, but incidental costs of arranging finance, such as mortgage broker fees are revenue expenses.

See Chapter 12 – Capital Gains Tax Basics on Page 185

8. Are capital repayments excluded from loan interest and other finance charges?

   See Chapter 7 – Mortgage and Finance Interest on Page 120

9. Check any expenses with a dual purpose, such as private use of a holiday property, are apportioned correctly.

   A common wrongly claimed expense here is life assurance against a buy to let mortgage, which has no business purpose and is disallowed from property business accounts.

   See Chapter 5 – Splitting Income And Expenses on Page 98

10. If a landlord claims travel for a vehicle owned by the business, has all commuting and other private use been excluded?

    Don't forget the same proportion of business mileage for a non-business vehicle should apply to any capital allowances if they are claimed against the vehicle.

    See Chapter 7 – Putting The Brakes On Travel on Page 113

11. Are all expenses in a non-business vehicle claimed by the landlord wholly and exclusively for the rental business?

    Tax inspectors specifically check trips abroad to split the costs between private and business use unless the sole purpose of the trip is for business.

    See Chapter 7 – Putting The Brakes On Travel on Page 113

12. If a landlord pays wages and salary, does the business have a PAYE scheme and have all income tax and national insurance contributions (NICs) been paid correctly?

Tax inspectors are told to check PAYE and NICs are deducted from payments made to any non-owner employed in the business.

See Chapter 7 – Paying Property Business Wages on Page 123

13. If wages or salaries are paid to relatives or connected persons, are the payments commensurate with their duties?

    Like many of these checks, this is a tax avoidance issue aimed at stopping landlords siphoning off money through family members and the claiming them as deductions against rental profits.

    See Chapter 7 – Paying Property Business Wages on Page 123

14. If a property has been let rent free or at less than normal market rate (an uncommercial let), have business expenses been restricted accordingly?

    Technically, if a property is not let at a commercial rent, it is not a letting property, so no business expenses can be set against the income.

    See Chapter 3 – Understanding Uncommercial Lets on Page 69

15. If the portfolio includes furnished letting property, has the 10% Wear and Tear Allowance been calculated correctly?

    Do not claim the allowance for unfurnished homes, furnished holiday lets or property owned by a company – claim capital allowances instead.

    See Chapter 8 – Calculating Out Wear-And-Tear Allowance on Page 131

16. If Rent-A-Room Relief is claimed does it meet the qualifying conditions?

    Rent-A-Room Relief only applies if the householder is living in the property and the room is let to a lodger, not for business or storage.

Check the claim meets rental income thresholds.

See Chapter 17 on page 250

17. Treat any income over the Rent-A-Room limit as taxable rental income.

See Page 252

18. Check that capital allowances are only claimed for holiday lets, communal areas in a house in multiple occupation (HMO) or for plant and machinery in general business use.

See Chapter 9 – Cut Tax With Capital Allowances on Page 140

19. Are the receipts and expenses tied to the April 6 – April 5 basis period?

If not, the receipts and expenses need to be apportioned to the financial year.

See Chapter 4 – Accounting Periods on Page 81

20. Check any rental business losses are offset in full against the first available rental profits and are applied to the correct rental business.

See Chapter 8 – Property Business Losses on Page 137

21. Has any tax been deducted from the rental payments of non-resident landlords?

See Chapter 19 Non-Resident Landlord Tax

22. If Box 21 in the SA105 property pages of the self-assessment return is completed, have the correct figures been included at Box 20?

Box 21 would include figures such as tax deducted

from the UK rents of non-resident landlords.

Box 20 should reflect the gross rental income of the business – which is the rent received plus any tax or other deductions. To avoid confusion a working showing how the gross rental figure was reached could be included in the additional information box on the core SA100 tax return.

Download the Property Rental Toolkit – http://www.hmrc.gov.uk/agents/toolkits/property-rental.pdf

Watching Your Personal Spending

1. Review property expenses to identify and remove any business spending related to personal use of property.

   HMRC will look at expenses to ensure profits are not understated by including personal transactions as business spending.

   Specific expenses tax inspectors target include travel, repairs that might be capital expenses and private use of holiday lets.

   See Splitting Income And Expenses on Page 98

2. Does credit card analysis include any personal spending?

   Tax inspectors will go through statements to try to identify private transactions classified as business spending. The best way of accounting for credit card spending is to allocate a card for a property business.

   Interest or late payment fees charged by card providers should be apportioned according to the proportion of private and business spending on the card.

   See Debit, Credit and Store Cards on Page 122

3. If a property investor works from a home office,

has the area of the home used for business been identified?

Calculate your home as office expenses with our special template and attach the bills to qualify the claim if HMRC asks how the figure was calculated.

See Home Office Costs on Page 115

4. If a vehicle owned by the business is used for non-business travel, including trips from home to work, only claim the business travel.

   Some property businesses own a van or car. If the landlord works from home and travels in the vehicle, some trips will be commuting and others might be for private purposes.

   These costs have to be separated out from business travel. A tax inspector will expect to see a mileage log for the vehicle that accurately records business travel during the tax year.

   If capital allowances are claimed for the vehicle, they must be apportioned so the claim does not include any personal use of the vehicle.

See Page 113, Putting The Brakes On Travel

5. If a private vehicle is used for business, check any claim relates solely to business travel.

   A tax inspector will expect to see a mileage log for the vehicle that accurately records business travel during the tax year.

See Page 113, Putting The Brakes On Travel

6. If a property owner takes a spouse or relative on business trips, are their personal costs excluded from expenses claims?

   If the spouse or relative is not a joint property owner with you but their travel was for a business purpose concerning your property, then the travel costs can be claimed in full. If not, make sure their share of the cost of any trip remains unclaimed.

See the Wholly and Exclusively Rule on Page 97

7. Are all expenses claimed for meals and subsistence wholly and exclusively for business purposes?

   The cost of food and drink is not generally wholly and exclusively for business and therefore normally not allowable.

See Meals And Staying Overnight on Page 114

8. Have profits been adjusted for the costs of any entertaining, gifts and sponsorship?

   Entertaining costs, including travelling to and from an event, are not allowed.

   Claims for the cost of gifts are only allowed if the gift is for advertising. Small gifts such as pens, diaries and key rings carrying an 'obvious advert' are allowed.

   If a landlord makes a gift, donation or subscription to a charity other than solely for business purposes, no claim is allowed.

   Sponsorship offered to a relative or friend of a landlord or when the landlord has a personal interest in the sponsored activity is not allowed.

9. If wages or salaries are paid to relatives or connected persons are the amounts related to the work they carried out?

   Non-owners can be paid for work they do for landlords, but the payment has to relate to the commercial rate for the work they do.

   Don't forget if you pay wages, the business should run a HMRC PAYE scheme.

See Paying Property Business Wages on Page 123

Download the Personal Expenses Toolkit – http://www.hmrc.gov.uk/agents/toolkits/capital-v-revenue.pdf

Accounting For Capital Costs

1. Has all capital spending been identified and allocated correctly?

   If a new property is not suitable for a tenant to move into, then spending on refurbishment may be a capital cost. It's important to separate capital costs from day-to-day business spending.

   See Chapter 6 for more about capital expenses

2. Has any incidental expenditure relating to buying or disposing of a property been properly accounted for?

   These costs are capital costs and should be held on a property register and included in a capital gains tax return.

   See Chapter 6 on Page 102

Download the Capital Expenses Toolkit – http://www.hmrc.gov.uk/agents/toolkits/capital-v-revenue.pdf

Checking Capital Allowances

1. If the business has disposed of any plant or machinery, make sure the amount if offset as a balancing charge.

   Keep a list of any disposals in the tax year along with any receipts for money received.

   See Balancing Charges on Page 145

2. Have all business assets used for non-business purposes been identified?

   HMRC will target any capital allowances claimed for private use of business-owned vehicles.

One issue is when a business-owned vehicle is used for trips between home and work. Sometimes they check computers for personal use, such as gaming software.

If plant or equipment has a dual business and private use, split the capital allowance claim accordingly.

See Splitting Income And Expenses on Page 98

3. Watch for double claims – a common one is mileage allowance paid to someone driving a vehicle for which capital allowances have been claimed.

   If mileage allowance is claimed, the vehicle is probably not owned by the business, so a capital allowance claim is not valid.

   Capital allowances and mileage claims are either/or reliefs.

Download the Capital Allowances Toolkit – http://www.hmrc.gov.uk/agents/toolkits/ca-plant-machinery.pdf

Action List

- ☑ Use this list to double check the points that trigger tax inquiries from HMRC on the SA105 Property Pages or SA106 Foreign Pages of your self-assessment tax return
- ☑ You can use this list and the information about landlord expenses to make sure you are claiming all available tax reliefs and allowances for your property business
- ☑ Don't forget HMRC is clamping down on travel and private costs treated as business expenses, so pay special attention to any payments that could fall under either of these categories

Part III

All About Capital Gains Tax

Property investors have a fear of capital gains tax, but this part of the book helps tame the beast. Capital gains tax is generally nowhere near as bad as people believe because they do not understand and take into account the available reliefs and allowances

Chapter 12

Capital Gains Tax Basics

Chapter preview:

- Understanding CGT jargon
- Who pays CGT and how much?
- Calculating your CGT bill
- Gifting property & CGT
- Separation, divorce and CGT
- Dealing with CGT losses

Capital Gains Tax or CGT is the second major tax besides income tax that landlords have to factor into their finances.

CGT is charged on the disposal of homes in a letting business – and disposal can include the sale or gifting of a part or all of the property.

The tax is levied on the 'chargeable gain'.

This is the appreciation in value of the property from the date of purchase less the buying price, any capital losses and several important expenses.

CGT is only an issue for long-term property investors.

Speculators or developers buying property to turn around for a quick profit do not pay CGT on their profits, but income tax.

See Page 256 for more about taxes paid by buy to sell property developers

Understanding CGT Jargon

CGT comes with a list of specialist terms that are included in HM Revenue & Customs (HMRC) CGT tax returns and guidance.

Here are explanations of some of the most common terms:

Basis of assessment – CGT is applied to the tax year when the disposal was made.

Chargeable gain – A chargeable gain is the proceeds of a disposal, less capital expenses and any capital losses. A key point is CGT is only levied once a disposal is made.

Disposal – For property tax, a disposal is:

- The sale of all or part of an asset – for example, selling a buy to let home or a piece of land from a larger plot
- Gifting the property
- Destruction of the property

Special rules govern transferring ownership between spouses or civil partners, which is CGT exempt.

See Page 190 for more about inter-spouse transfers

Principle Residence Relief (PRR) – The disposal of an individual's main home is exempt from CGT.

See Page 205 for more about PRR

Annual exempt amount (AEA) – The annual exempt amount works in the same way as the personal income tax allowance.

Everyone has an annual exempt amount, which is lost if unused. The annual exempt amount is deducted from a chargeable gain before tax due is calculated.

See Page 187 for CGT tax rates

Who Pays CGT And How Much?

The beneficial owner pays capital gains tax – that's the person who is entitled to some or all of the proceeds from a disposal.

Read more about beneficial ownership on Page 52

A property owner does not have to report a property disposal on a tax return if:

- There's no tax to pay
- Total sale proceeds in the tax year are less than four times the annual exempt amount

This last exception is rarely used as property prices in most parts of the country have outstripped the limit, which is £44,000 for 2014-15.

Nevertheless, it's worth bearing in mind for income shifting to save on CGT.

See Page 193 for more about CGT and income shifting

Calculating Your Capital Gains Tax Bill

Income tax and CGT are separate taxes, but conveniently, CGT uses the same basic and higher rate income bandings for allocating lower and higher rates of capital gains tax.

CGT is paid on gains within the basic rate band at 18% and at 28% in the higher or additional rate band.

If the taxpayer is already a higher or additional rate taxpayer, then gains are always charged at 28%.

For basic rate taxpayers with unused income in their banding, the taxable gain is split, with the part in the basic rate banding charged at 18% and the rest charged at 28%.

Here's a worked example:

In 2014-15, Peter has a taxable income of £25,000 after subtracting his personal allowance and a capital gain of £30,000 before deducting his annual exempt amount.

His taxable gain is £25,000 less his annual exempt amount of £11,000, which is £14,000.

He has £31,865 less £25,000 left in his basic rate tax banding, which is £6,865.

£6,865 of his gain is taxed at 18% and the balance at 28%, so Peter's capital gains tax bill is:

- £6,865 x 18% = £1,235.70
- £7,135 x 28% = £1,997.80
- The total CGT bill is £3,233.50

Establishing date of ownership

CGT is calculated between two key dates – the date you took on unconditional ownership of the property and the date you handed that unconditional ownership to someone else.

This is not necessarily the same as the date of completion.

For example, Tim signs the unconditional contract for a property purchase on April 6, 2005, and completes the purchase on April 13, 2005.

He then sells the property, signing the unconditional contract on April 1, 2014, but the sale does not complete until April 30, 2014. Tim pays CGT based on the value of the property on April 6, 2005, and the disposal proceeds he received for the completion.

However, the tax point for the transaction is April 1, 2014. The transaction is included in his 2014-15 tax return with any CGT due to be paid on January 31, 2015.

Each disposal is calculated separately, so if a property investor sells a rental home and some shares, the calculations are separate, but the losses of one can be set off against the gain of the other.

Once each calculation is completed, the taxable amounts are

CGT Computation Pro Forma

	£	£
Disposal proceeds		x
Less		
Incidental disposal costs		(x)
Net proceeds		x
Less		
Original cost	x	
Incidental acquisition costs	x	
Improvement costs	x	
Costs of defending title	x	
Total costs		(x)
Chargeable gain or loss		**x**

added up, the annual exempt amount deducted and the CGT calculated against basic and higher rate tax as in the example above (Peter).

Now, let's go through each category of the computation step-by-step explaining what is included, followed by a worked example.

Disposal proceeds

For landlords selling an investment property, the disposal proceeds are easy to work out – it's all the cash raised from the sale before deducting any expenses.

However, two exceptions apply:

> **Gifted or sold to a connected person -** If the property was gifted to anyone or sold to a 'connected person' at less than market value, then CGT rules

deem the transaction took place at market value regardless of the price the property agreed between the individuals concerned.

From this, you can see a chargeable gain can arise from a property transaction even if no money has changed hands.

If the gift results in a loss, the loss is only offset against other gains on disposals to the same connected person.

Setting the market value is straightforward – a surveyor's valuation will give the price. If HMRC disputes the valuation, the Valuation Office steps in.

The Valuation Office acts on the same guidelines provided by the Royal Institution of Chartered Surveyors to private surveyors to produce an independent property valuation.

If the property is destroyed – for example, demolished to make way for redevelopment or suffers a gas explosion – then the disposal is for nothing and zero is the figure entered in the computation.

Sometimes this may be a loss if the costs of site clearance are taken into account.

However, if an insurance pay-out is received, the claim proceeds become the disposal value.

Disposals to spouses or civil partners

Following the principle that married couples can arrange their finances as they see fit to minimise the tax they pay, any property transferred to a spouse or civil partner is rated at zero for CGT purposes. This is generally called a 'no gain, no loss' transfer.

For example, Wendy buys a buy to let property for £50,000 in 2001.

In 2010, she transfers the ownership to her husband, Donald. The disposal proceeds are deemed as zero under the 'no gain, no loss' rule.

In 2015, Donald sells the property. His base cost – the original cost of the property for CGT – is the £50,000 Wendy paid to buy the home.

Transfers to 'connected people'

The connected people rules are designed to stop owners passing investment properties around their families to gain a tax advantage.

Here's a list of connected people – but don't forget their relatives, spouses or civil partners are also connected people as well:

- Husbands, wives and civil partners
- Parents, grandparents and great-grandparents etc
- Brothers and sisters
- Children, grandchildren and great-grandchildren etc
- In-laws
- Business partners – but not joint property owners
- Any company you control or a person connected to you controls
- Any trust where you or a connected person is a beneficiary

Lineal descendants are always connected people – so uncles, aunts, nephews, nieces and cousins are not included in the list but step-relatives are.

Incidental disposal costs

Unlike property revenue expenses, strict rules govern the expenses a property owner can offset against a chargeable gain.

These expenses are set out in Section 38 of the Taxation of Chargeable Gains Act 1992. For a disposal, these costs are:

- Marketing – Costs related to estate agents, auctions or advertising property for sale

- Legal fees – Lawyer's charges for the conveyancing, including money transfers and related costs

- Professional costs – Any charges involved in valuing the property for CGT purposes

Original or base cost

The price paid for the property or the market value on the transfer date. Sometimes the original cost is calculated in line with a specific date.

March 31, 1982 is a special date for CGT. If you owned the property before this date, CGT is worked out according to the valuation on March 31, 1982, regardless of the purchase date and value.

If you inherited the property, the valuation on the date of death of the deceased who left you the property is the original cost for CGT purposes.

Incidental acquisition costs

Like incidental disposal costs, these are also set out in Section 38 of the Taxation of Chargeable Gains Act 1992.

These costs are:

- Professional fees – Any money paid to a surveyor, auctioneer, accountant or other professional involved in the acquisition of the property. Other professionals could include specialists, like a structural engineer

- Legal fees – Lawyer's charges for the conveyancing, including money transfers and related costs

- Stamp duty

Improvement costs

Improvement costs, or capital expenses, are tax reducers – every pound spent knocks a pound of your chargeable gain. From the date of acquisition – the day you took over unconditional control of the property – start keeping a capital expenses register.

You should start with a comprehensive video or image gallery of the property to prove exactly what standard the fixtures and fittings of the property were like on the day of purchase.

At some point, you may want to change the kitchen or bathroom and need to prove if the work is a repair or an improvement.

As a landlord, you want an instant return as a revenue expense rather than holding a capital expense on your property register for years.

Revenue costs reduce your rental profits and the benefit is passed on immediately, while capital costs only crystallise on the disposal of a property, so classify the expense correctly.

What are improvements?

Generally, improvements are adding something new to a property or upgrading to a better standard.

Repairs and maintenance are considered as a like-for-like replacement of something that is already there.

So, replacing roof tiles blown off in a storm or even reroofing a property are repairs, but replacing the roof with a loft extension is an improvement that adds value to the property.

Bills for improvements should be kept from day one of ownership for inclusion in any potential capital gains tax computation.

For a detailed explanation of the difference between capital and revenue expenses, see Chapter 6

Costs of defending title

Costs of defending your title to the property would cover issues such as lawyer's fees relating to a boundary dispute, a disagreement over a right of way, or defending a legal challenge against your right of ownership.

Saving CGT With Income Shifting

Now you have been through the basic format for a capital gains tax calculation, it's time to look at a worked example.

Robert and Allison bought a buy to let home in September 2001 for £95,000. The legal fees were £990 and stamp duty of £550 was paid.

In May 2014, the couple sold the property for £275,000. They paid an estate agent £3,500 to arrange the sale and legal fees of £780.

During the time they owned the property, they added an extension costing £8,500 which was still in place when they exchanged contracts for the sale.

They did not dispose of any other assets in the tax year.

Robert is a higher rate (40%) taxpayer, while Allison is a basic rate taxpayer (20%), earning £21,500 a year.

This is how to calculate their CGT bill:

After working out the chargeable gain, the next step is to split the gain according to each owner's percentage share of the property.

	£	£
Disposal proceeds:		275,000
Less		
Incidental disposal costs:		(4,280)
Net proceeds:		270,720
Less		
Purchase value:	95,000	
Incidental acquisition costs	8,500	
Improvement costs	8,500	
Cost of defending title	0	
		(105,040)
Chargeable gain:		165,680

Robert and Allison are joint tenants holding a 50% share each, so their CGT liability is calculated by dividing the chargeable gain according to each owner's share.

This is calculated as £165,680 x 50% = £82,840.

As there are no allowed losses, next subtract the annual exempt amount of £11,000 for each to arrive at the net chargeable gain - this is the figure any tax due is calculated against and varies from year to year.

So £82,840 - £11,000 = £71,840

Robert's CGT liability

As Robert is a higher rate taxpayer, CGT on his net chargeable gain is all charged at 28%.

That's £71,840 x 28% = £20,115

Allison's CGT liability

Allison is a basic rate taxpayer. To calculate her CGT, top-up her basic rate earnings to the higher rate limit.

She can earn £41,865 a year at the basic rate, including her £10,000 tax-free personal income tax allowance.

Allison earns £21,500, so she can take the balance of £20,365 (£41,865 - £21,500) from her chargeable gain to be taxed at 18%. The balance is charged at 28%.

Her CGT is calculated as:

- £20,365 x 18% = £3,665
- £51,475 x 28% = £14,413

The total CGT Allison pays is £18,078

The £51,475 comes from taking the £71,840 net chargeable gain less £20,365, which is the balance of her earnings charged at basic rate income tax.

 In Chapter 2, income shifting to save income tax on rental profits

was explained, but do not forget the same principle applies to capital gains tax as well.

How CGT income shifting works

In the previous example, if Robert had owned the house outright, his capital gains tax liability would have been completely different.

His chargeable gain less his annual exempt amount would have been £165,680 less £11,000, leaving a net chargeable gain of £154,680.

Robert's tax would then be £154,680 x 28%, which is a massive £43,310.

After income shifting with Allison, his tax reduced to £20,115 and Allison paid £18,078, making a total of £38,193.

That adds up to a capital gains tax saving of £5,117 simply by shifting a share of the property between spouses.

Remember, whenever spouses or civil partners pay income tax at different rates, an opportunity to income shift and save money opens up.

Always run the numbers by calculating how much income shifting might save in tax paid. Don't forget to factor in the costs of transferring ownership.

Gifting Property And CGT

Capital gains tax on gifting property depends on who the property goes to and the value of the gift.

Another tax pitfall relating to gifting property is inheritance tax.

Gifting property is a 'potential exempt transfer' or PET for inheritance tax purposes.

The potential is the gift is free from IHT providing the donor lives seven years after making a gift, no inheritance tax is due.

During the intervening period, the amount of tax decreases on a sliding scale each year. For IHT purposes, a gift must be unconditional, so retaining any sort of control means no disposal has taken place, therefore no tax is due.

Gifts to a spouse or civil partner

Switching property ownership between spouses or civil partners is a 'no gain, no loss' transfer, so no capital gains tax is triggered by the disposal, providing:

- Both spouses or civil partners lived together for at least part of the tax year in which the gift was made
- The gift is not trading property bought for resale

However, if your spouse or civil partner later disposes of the property, they'll have to pay tax on any gain.

Tax will be due on any gain made over the total period of ownership since March 31, 1982 by both spouses.

No CGT is due on gains on property bought before this date.

Gifts to relatives and 'connected people'

Capital gains tax is paid on any gift to a relative or another person you're connected with other than a spouse or civil partner.

This also applies if you dispose of a property to them in any other way – such as selling at a reduced price.

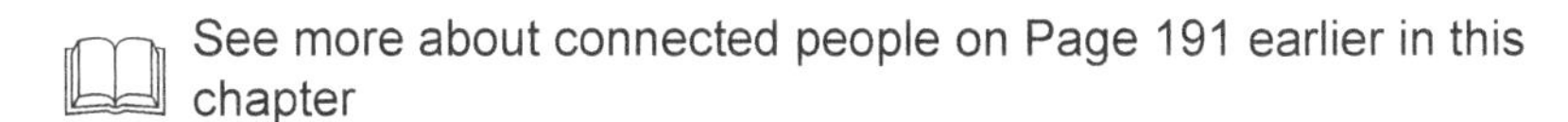
See more about connected people on Page 191 earlier in this chapter

Property transfers to connected people are deemed to take place at open market value, regardless of the price paid.

If you make a loss, you can only offset the loss from other gains you make on other disposals to the same connected person.

Gifts to charity

Capital gains tax is not always due on property gifts to a UK registered charity. This is specialist advice which should be discussed with a tax professional or lawyer.

Death, inheritance and capital gains tax

When someone dies, the properties they own pass to an executor or personal representative administrating their estate. No capital gains tax is due at that time, even though the property has changed hands.

If someone inherits the property, no capital gains tax is due, although the estate may have to pay inheritance tax.

However, on disposal of the property, the new owner may have to pay capital gains tax on any gain they may have made.

The base cost for capital gains tax becomes the value of the property on the date the former owner died.

This should be evidenced by a valuation the estate administrator commissioned when working out the value of the estate for inheritance tax.

Separation, Divorce And CGT

Sometimes when you separate, divorce or dissolve a civil partnership, you need to transfer property between partners.

Whether any capital gains tax is due depends on when the transfer took place -

- In the tax year of separation
- After the tax year separation
- After divorce or dissolution of a civil partnership

Transfers in the tax year of separation

If you transfer property to a spouse or civil partner in the tax year when separation took place, then the same rules apply as for gifts between spouses.

 See the section above 'Gifts to a spouse or civil partner'

You won't have to pay capital gains tax if:

- You lived together for at least some of that tax year

  AND

- The gift isn't a buy to sell property

Transfers in the tax year after separation

You will have to work out any capital gain or loss if you transfer property to a spouse or civil partner in the tax year after separation if the following rules apply:

- You transfer any property between yourselves other than your main home

  AND

- You've been separated for the complete tax year

  AND

- You're not divorced or your civil partnership has not been dissolved

Value the property on the date of the transfer and use this value as the proceeds to work out the gain or loss.

If you transfer your home to your spouse or civil partner, the gain is covered by private residence relief (PRR).

Transfers after divorce

Calculating capital gains tax on transferring property after a divorce or dissolution of a civil partnership is no easy task and should be undertaken by a tax professional.

You adviser will need to know:

- The date of the decree absolute or dissolution

- If property was transferred under a court order, the date and details of the order

- The date of any other contract showing when any property was transferred

If you transfer your home to your spouse or civil partner, the gain is covered by private residence relief (PRR).

Dealing With CGT Losses

Allowed losses are offset against other capital gains in the same tax year or future years.

Losses are called 'allowed' because taxpayers have to have permission from HMRC before including a loss in any CGT computation.

Losses arise when a property is disposed of for less than the buying price plus incidental costs and any capital expenses incurred.

How to claim a loss

To offset a loss, a property owner has to tell HMRC about the loss within a strict time limit.

Normally, this is done by completing the SA108 capital gains pages of a self-assessment tax return. Property owners who may not complete a tax return should send the details to HMRC in a letter.

The deadline for notification is four years from the end of the year of assessment.

For example, if you made a loss on the disposal of a buy to let home in June 2014, the end of the year of assessment is April 5, 2015. The notification needs to arrive with HMRC on or before April 5, 2019.

Deducting losses from your capital gains

Don't forget other losses can be deducted from a gain on the disposal of a property. For example, disposals of shares that have lost value - then losses are offset against a chargeable gain in a set order: –

- Bring forward any unused allowed losses from between the 1996-97 tax year to date and add them to any allowed losses made in the current tax year.

- Cancel out any chargeable gain pound for pound in the current tax year after deducting the annual exempt amount.

  The annual exempt amount is a tax-free allowance, so include this in your computation to conserve losses to offset against future gains.

  But add the amount back on your tax return as HMRC will automatically deduct the relief, otherwise you claim twice and distort the tax computation.

- If you still have a chargeable gain and unused losses from 1995-96 or earlier, bring them forward at this point and offset them against any further chargeable gain.

- If your losses are still more than your chargeable gain in the tax year, carry them forward to the next tax year when you make a gain and go through the same steps again.

Here's a worked example for offsetting allowed losses.

In January 2014, David sells two buy to let homes and makes a loss of £20,000 on one and a gain of £75,000 on the other.

David has also brought forward an allowed loss of £64,000 from the 2010-11 tax year.

To work out his chargeable gain, David first subtracts his current year loss of £20,000 from the current year gain of £75,000, leaving a net gain of £55,000.

Now, David takes his brought forward loss from previous tax years to reduce the gain to his annual exempt amount of £10,900. The £10,900 is his annual exempt amount which will be deducted by HMRC.

That's £55,000 less £10,900, leaving £44,100.

£64,000 less £44,100 is £19,900.

That leaves £19,900 as the balance of unused allowed losses for David to carry forward to offset against his next available chargeable gain.

Action List

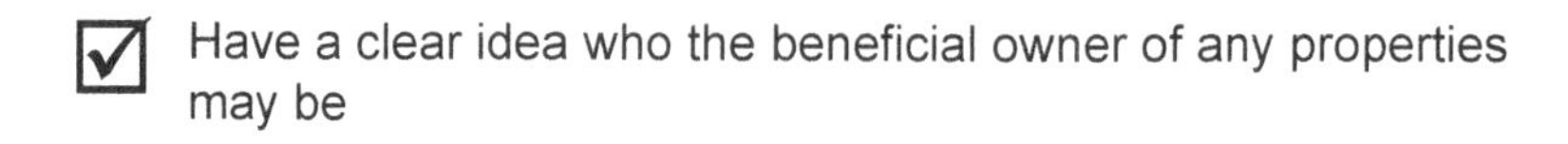

- ☑ Have a clear idea who the beneficial owner of any properties may be
- ☑ Look at income shifting between spouses or civil partners to save capital gains tax before exchanging contracts on any property disposal
- ☑ If you are separated or divorcing, keep an eye on the time limits for tax-free property transfers
- ☑ Make sure any capital losses are registered with HM Revenue & Customs within the four year limit - and don't forget you can offset other losses such as shares against property disposals

Chapter 13

Special CGT Rules For Landlords

Chapter preview:

- Handling part disposals of property
- Private Residence Relief (PRR)
- Calculating PRR
- Lettings Relief
- Entrepreneur's Relief

This chapter looks at some unique capital gains tax rules that apply to homeowners and property investors.

The main concern of this chapter is what happens when a property investor has lived in a home of which they are disposing or is only disposing of part of a property.

Besides highlighting some of the problems, we will also show there are some solutions to ensure property owners do not fall into some of the expensive pitfalls that can come with claiming capital gains tax reliefs on the sale of a home.

To help with this, we will review some of the latest tax tribunal cases that throw some light on how tax inspectors view claiming Private Residence Relief (PRR) on property disposals.

Lastly, there's a quick look at Entrepreneur's Relief, which is a reduced rate of capital gains tax for owners of furnished holiday lets, relief which is only available if the property meets some strict rules.

Handling Part Disposals Of Property

As we saw in the previous chapter, capital gains tax involves disposing of all or part of a property.

The most common scenario for a part disposal of property is when a piece of land is sold to a neighbour or developer.

From a tax standpoint, if a property is owned as a single title and part of that property is detached from the title and disposed of to someone else, then the gain of loss for that specific transaction needs to be calculated.

The issue is that the property owner will know the original cost of the property, but not how much of the purchase and sale prices relate to the disposal.

Our old maths favourite apportionment is the answer. In Chapter 5, we saw how income and expenses are apportioned according to business use and ownership. Part disposals are handled the same way, by valuing the asset on disposal and then apportioning the cost.

The calculation comes down to a simple formula:

$$\text{Original cost of entire asset} \quad = \quad \frac{A}{A+B}$$

WHERE

A = Proceeds or market value of the disposal

B = Market value of the part of the asset kept

Here's a worked example going through the formula step-by step:

Michael bought a piece of land in January 1995 for £3,000.

In April 2014, he sold part of the land for £4,000, while the value of the remainder of the land at the time of disposal was set at £12,000.

So, we first work out the original cost of part disposal:

£3,000 (Original cost) x £4,000 (Part disposal proceeds) divided by £4,000 plus £12,000 (Value of retained land)

That works out as £3,000 x £4,000/£16,000 = £750

The chargeable gain is then:

Proceeds	£4,000
Less cost	(£750)
Chargeable gain:	£3,250

This is a much simplified capital gains tax computation, as we would also need to apportion any acquisition, improvement and disposal costs to the same formula to set off against the gain.

Private Residence Relief (PRR)

Sometimes call Principal Residence Relief, PRR is the major capital gains tax reducer for property investors who have spent some time living in a buy to let home which they are selling or gifting to someone other than their spouse.

The intention of the tax rule is to exempt homeowners from paying capital gains tax when they dispose of their main home and to apportion the relief if the home has been let.

PRR also provides a sometimes controversial relief for a property investor who has sold a home they have lived in for only a short time.

How does PRR work?

The relief applies on the disposal of:

- A home, which can include a house, flat, houseboat or static caravan

  OR

- Part of a home

  OR

- Part of the garden attached to a home

PROVIDING

- The home has been your only or main residence throughout the time of ownership

AND

- You have not lived elsewhere, other than for an allowed period of absence or because you have had job-related accommodation during your period of ownership

AND

- The garden or grounds including the buildings on them are not greater than the permitted area (Half a hectare)

AND

- No part of your home has been used exclusively for business while you have lived there

Tax traps

HM Revenue & Customs (HMRC) guidance on capital gains tax warns that if a homeowner sells the property but keeps part of the garden and later sells that land, PRR does not apply to the sale of the land.

The tax-effective way to do this is to sell off plots carved off the original title before selling your home otherwise PRR will not apply to subsequent disposals.

HMRC cautions that capital gains tax and PRR does not apply to buying a home to sell on as quickly as possible.

This is considered a buy to sell and income tax is applied to any profits.

See Chapter 18 for more about buy to sell and developing

Lastly, if part of a garden is fenced off in such a way that it cannot be used for the enjoyment of the homeowner, that part of the property does not qualify for PRR either.

An example would be fencing off part of a garden for a neighbour's exclusive use. The neighbour does not have to pay a rent or to buy the land, just to have exclusive use.

PRR terms defined

Let's address the elephant in the room first. How long do you have to live in an investment property to make it your main home and qualify for PRR relief?

The answer is not simple – it depends.

It's not the length or the 'quantity' of occupation, it's all about the 'quality' of occupation.

The most recent tax tribunal cases ruling on the question are:

Moore v HMRC [2013] TC02827
http://www.bailii.org/cgi-bin/markup.cgi?doc=/uk/cases/UKFTT/TC/2013/TC02827.html

In the Piers Moore case, the tax tribunal was asked to decide whether the three months he spent living in the house while refurbishing the property as a buy to let made the property his main residence.

Moore could produce no evidence to show he had moved in and HMRC offered evidence that three years later he had moved into another property and claimed he lived there for a few weeks while refurbishing that as a buy to let as well.

The issue at stake was Moore was disputing a capital gains tax bill of almost £14,500 on the grounds he had three months plus 36 months PRR that exempted the amount.

The tribunal found against him on the grounds that his mail and bills were all delivered to other addresses and his claim was not supported by any evidence.

A point worth noting is Moore had informed HMRC that the buy to let was his main address, but the tribunal found that action alone was not sufficient to prove the matter.

Dr S Iles and Dr D Kaltsas v HMRC [2014] TC03565
LINK: http://www.bailii.org/cgi-bin/markup.cgi?doc=/uk/cases/UKFTT/TC/2014/TC03565.html

Susan Iles and Dimitris Kaltsas also lost their case before a tax tribunal when claiming that living in a flat for just 25 days prior to selling the property gave them 36 months and 25 days of PRR.

The tribunal felt moving in was just a stop gap by the owners to try and avoid capital gains tax because the home was already for sale when they moved in.

The definitive case on residence for PRR is considered to be *Goodwin v Curtis [1998] (70TC478)*, which went to the Court of Appeal.

Mr Goodwin bought a farmhouse but put the property up for sale before moving in.

He had separated from his wife and moved in on April 1, 1985 and sold the property on May 3, 1985 – 32 days in total.

The tribunal rejected Goodwin's claim for PRR on the grounds that the property could never have been his permanent home because he intended to sell.

In the Court of Appeal, Lord Justice Millett said: "The quality of the taxpayer's occupation of the farmhouse did not have a sufficient degree of permanence, continuity or expectation of continuity to justify its description as residence.

"Temporary occupation at an address does not make a man resident there."

Lord Justice Schiemann added: "In order to qualify for private residence relief a taxpayer must provide some evidence that his residence in the property showed some degree of permanence, some degree of continuity or some expectation of continuity."

Living away from home

Homeowners can still claim PRR if they have spent some extended periods of time living away from their home for specific reasons.

The three qualifying periods of absence are:

- Absence for any reason of no more than three years during the time the property is owned
- Absence because your job takes you outside the UK
- Absences of no more than four years when
  - The commuting distance between home and work is too far to be reasonable

    OR

  - Your employer requires you to work away from home to do your job

In each case, the home owner is expected to live in the property immediately before and after the absence. Also note that the rule also applies if you live elsewhere because of your spouse's job.

Job-related accommodation

If your employer offers accommodation and you also own a home in which you intend to live, that home qualifies for PRR even if you never live there – but if you move in tenants, PRR stops.

Grounds for concern

HMRC follows a half a hectare rule for how far private residence relief can be extended into the grounds of homes with larger gardens or land around them.

The rule includes buildings that stand on the land, so if you have a garden of half a hectare with a cottage as well as your own home and you sell the cottage, then PRR covers the sale.

The rule is there to combat tax avoidance. For instance, if someone owns a farm extending over 100 acres, only the land necessary to enjoy the garden and surroundings around their home is covered by PRR, not the entire 100 acres.

If you have a large home, you can argue with HMRC that the property ought to have a larger PRR plot around it, providing you can show how the land is used.

Although the rule is there to deter tax avoidance, genuine homeowners can also take the same legislation to help improve their tax position as well.

Some home owners have convinced tax inspectors that they ought to have more land as their PRR allowance. In most of these cases, they have lived in an area where their neighbours have had large homes with sizeable gardens and grounds.

A tax trigger to note is any land which is fenced off or on which preliminary development work has started on the date of disposal is excluded from PRR.

Calculating Private Residence Relief

If a property owner only lives in the home as their main residence for part of their period of ownership, then PRR is apportioned to cover that time only.

The formula is:

$$\text{Total gain} \times \frac{\text{Period of occupation as main home}}{\text{Period of ownership}}$$

Here are calculations for a sole owner and a married couple:

CGT computation - sole owner

Phillip bought a house in Southampton in January 2001 for £200,000 and lived in the property as his main residence until January 2002, when he had a cash windfall that allowed him to buy a larger property in Winchester.

Phillip kept his Southampton home, but rented it out as a buy to let while living in Winchester. In January 2014, he decided to sell the Southampton property, for which he received £400,000.

The buying and selling costs were £5,000 and £3,000. During his period of ownership, Phillip also spent £20,000 on improving the property. In the 2014-15 tax year, Phillip earned £45,000, making him a higher rate taxpayer.

How much capital gains tax does Phillip pay?

	£	£
Proceeds of disposal		400,000
Less		
Purchase price	200,000	
Acquisition costs	5,000	
Disposal costs	3,000	
Improvement costs	20,000	
		(228,000)
Net gain		**172,000**
Less		
PRR (Working 1)	52,923	
Lettings relief (Working 2)	40,000	
Annual exempt amount	11,000	
		(103,923)
Taxable gain		**68,077**
CGT tax due @ 28%		**19,061**

PRR - Working 1

A	Ownership (January 2001 - January 2014)	13 years
B	Main residence January 2011 - January 2002	1 year
C	Plus three years CGT exemption	3 years
D	Total period exempt from CGT (B+C)	4 years
E	CGT exempt gain (£172,000 x D/A)	£52,923
F	Gain chargeable to CGT (£172,000 x (A-D)/A	£119,077

Next, calculate Lettings Relief, but remember not to include the PRR three year exemption during the letting period as it has already been claimed under the PRR calculation.

Lettings Relief - Working 2

Lettings Relief is the lowest of:

Phillip's PRR exemption (Working 1 E):	£52,923
The maximum statutory Lettings Relief claim:	£40,000
The gain during the letting period:	£158,769

In this case, Lettings Relief is £40,000

CGT computation – married couple

Andrew and Beatrice bought a buy to let as joint tenants for £150,000 in April 2004, which they sold for £395,000 in April 2014. Andrew is a 40% taxpayer and Beatrice earns £15,000 a year, paying income tax at 20%.

They paid £5,000 in acquisition and disposal costs.

As Andrew and Beatrice are joint tenants, HMRC will assume ownership is 50:50 and will expect any rental profits and chargeable gains to be apportioned as such.

	£	£
Proceeds of disposal		395,000
Less		
Purchase price	150,000	
Acquisition costs	5,000	
Disposal costs	5,000	
		(160,000)
Net gain		**235,000**

Now the net gain is calculated, the next step is to split the gain according to proportion of ownership, and then to deduct each owner's annual exempt amount to leave their personal chargeable gain.

	Andrew	Beatrice
	£	£
Split gain 50:50	116,500	116,500
Less		
Annual exempt amount	(11,000)	(11,000)
Individual chargeable gain	106,500	106,500
CGT @ 18%	0	4,835
CGT @ 28%	29,820	22,297
CGT to pay:	29,820	27,132
Total CGT for Andrew and Beatrice		56,952

Working out Beatrice's CGT

Basic rate income threshold	41,865
Less income already charged at basic rate	(15,000)
Remaining income at charged at CGT basic rate	26,865
Chargeable gain charged at CGT higher rate (£106,500 - £26,865)	79,635

PRR change for UK residents

From April 6, 2014, the rule for PRR is changing.

For UK resident taxpayers, Instead of 36 months plus the time of residence being exempt from capital gains tax, the time will reduce to 18 months plus the time of residence.

The effect of this change is to reduce step C in the PRR calculations to 18 months.

CGT changes on the way - non-residents

For non-UK residents, April 6, 2015 also marks the end of tax-free residential property sales in Britain.

Until this date, a simple CGT tax saving strategy has been to build a portfolio of investment properties and then move overseas to become non-resident and sell them off without paying any tax in the UK.

From April 6, non-residents owning residential property in the UK will pay CGT on disposals in the same way as residents - but the gain will be assessed from that date.

This removes a big worry for some non-residents who may have held property for years that as bloated in value as the only gain that is assessable under the new rules is the gain from that date.

How the new rules work

From April 6, 2015, private residence relief is only available on an expat's former home if:

- The expat disposing of the home is tax resident in the same country as the property during the tax year when the disposal was made
- If the expat fails the first condition above, their spouse or civil partner can also meet the '90 midnight' rule – which means they have to overnight for 90 nights in the home or other homes they own in the same country during the tax year of the disposal

If one of the qualifying rules is met, the owner can claim 18 months private residence relief on top of any time they spent living in the home.

The 90 night rule

Should an expat have more than one home qualifying for private residence relief in the UK or spend more than 90 nights in a home they own in the UK, then they can nominate which is their main home.

This nomination is important and allows expats to minimise their

CGT bill by focusing their PRR on a single property.

However, some points need to be borne in mind.

- Nominating a main residence may make an expat tax resident in the UK and make all their worldwide income taxable in Britain
- Nominating a property strips private residence relief from any other properties during the same period, so it's wise to run some numbers before wasting this important relief on the wrong home
- Expats living in countries without a double taxation treaty with the UK may have to pay CGT in their home nation as well as the UK on the same disposal

Keeping financial records to prove the 90-day rule is vital for expats who want to claim private residence relief on the disposal of a home in the UK once they have moved overseas.

Not only is it important to prove the rule - but expats wanting to avoid UK tax residency need to show they fail to qualify as well.

HMRC suggests the best way of proving tax residence is keeping a diary of where and when expats stay alongside visa and other travel documents.

Expats living in countries without a double taxation treaty with the UK may also find they are due to pay CGT in their home nation as well as the UK on the same disposal.

Lettings Relief

The main point to remember about Lettings Relief is if a property has never been rented out, Lettings Relief does not apply.

If an owner lets out a property where they have lived, Lettings Relief applies: -

- Regardless of whether the letting was before or after the owner lived in the property
- To a property where the owner lives in one part and lets the rest

- If a property is jointly owned and let, when each owner can claim full Lettings Relief
- To each property not per owner or portfolio in a tax year

How much is Lettings Relief?

Lettings Relief is the lowest of:

- £40,000 - This is the statutory maximum Lettings Relief laid down in the Taxation of Chargeable Gains Act 1992
- The owner's PRR
- The capital gain made while the property was let

  The formula is:
  Ignore the three-year PRR exemption for Lettings relief as this is already claimed under the owner's PRR calculation

Here's an example to show how PRR and Lettings Relief work together. The figures show why the reliefs are important tax reducers.

The formula is:

$$\text{Total gain x } \frac{\text{Period of letting}}{\text{Period of ownership}}$$

Here's a worked example:

Marlene bought a two-bed house in May 2005 for £90,000 and lived there for a year.

Marlene then moved in with a new partner at another property and rented the house out as a buy to let until May 2014, when she sold the property for £200,000.

If Marlene has no other chargeable gains in the year, her annual exempt amount of £11,000 for the 2014-15 tax year means she would have capital gains tax to pay on the disposal, regardless of the profit she made.

	£	£
Proceeds of sale		200,000
Less		
Original cost		(90,000)
Net gain		**110,000**
Less		
PRR - Working 1	55,000	
Lettings Relief - Working 2	40,000	
		(95,000)
Chargeable gain		**5,000**

PRR - Working 1

A	Ownership	8 years
B	Period as main residence	1 year
C	Plus three years CGT exemption	3 years
D	Total period exempt from CGT (B+C)	4 years
E	CGT exempt gain (£110,000 x D/A)	£55,000
F	Gain chargeable to CGT (£110,000 x (A-D)/A	£55,000

Lettings Relief - Working 2

Marlene's PRR exemption (Working 1 E):	£55,000
Statutory maximum Lettings Relief	£40,000
Gain during letting period (£110,000 x 7/8):	£96,250

Main home elections

The government had planned to scrap 'flipping property' or main home elections after the bad press about the strategy following the scandal of MPs' expenses, but changed their mind. That means the opportunity to flip property is still available for investors.

The rules allow a married couple to only have one main home at a specific time to claim Private Residence Relief (PPR) against.

See Page 210 for more about calculating Private Residence Relief

How flipping saves CGT

If a couple has more than one home, shifting Principle Private Relief between them can reduce the amount of capital gains tax due on disposal.

Here's an example that shows how flipping works:

Keiron lives in a house in Stafford bought in 1994 for £100,000. In April 2001, he also bought a second home near the sea in Aberdyfi, Wales, for £250,000. The Aberdyfi home is for holidays and weekends away.

Keiron is coming up to retirement and wants to sell the home in Aberdyfi for £350,000.

However, as the Stafford property is his principle residence, Keiron has no relief to offset against the Aberdyfi property as HMRC will treat the Stafford property as his main home for the entire period of ownership.

The gain on the Aberdyfi property before allowable expenses and Keiron's annual exempt amount is £100,000.

As he is a higher rate taxpayer, the CGT will be £100,000, less £11,000 (the annual exempt amount) x 28%, which equals £24,920.

Keiron understands the flipping rules, so elected the Stafford property as his main home when he bought the Aberdyfi property.

Then, he flipped his main home to Aberdyfi by making another election in 2014.

From April 6, 2014, the election gives Keiron 18 months principle residence relief against CGT.

This gives him 18/144ths PPR to set off against his £100,000 gain, which reduces the taxable amount by £12,500 to £87,500.

In line with this, his CGT bill reduces to £21,450.

The calculations are:

PRR = £100,000 x (18/144) = £12,500

Taxable gain = 28% x (£100,000 (Gain) - £12,500 (PRR) - £11,000 (annual exempt amount))

Making a main home election

To flip your main home, simply write to your tax office and tell them what you are doing within two years of the date you acquired the property.

The time limit can be reset by either:

- Moving to a third property, which means the clock starts from the date of moving into the third home

  Or

- Letting one of the properties so it is excluded as a main residence and then moving back in, which restarts the two year countdown

Remember that married couples must both sign the election letter and the date of the letter is received by the tax office must fall within the two year limit.

The election is easily changed by filing a new main home nomination with the tax office.

A good point to remember is to nominate the property likely to be sold first or that will have the largest capital gain. Also, don't forget only one property can attract PRR at any one time.

No main home election

If you have more than one home and have not made an election, which becomes the main home is decided as a matter of fact.

The tax man will look at how much time is spent at each and where your main base is - this is decided by where you are registered to vote, where your bank statements and official post go and if you have children, where they live and go to school, for example.

How long is enough time to live in a main home?

This is an often argued point and generally comes down to looking at the facts like those in the previous paragraph.

The HMRC CGT manual guidance for tax inspectors says the election only has to last for a 'short space of time'

LINK: http//:www.hmrc.gov.uk/manuals/cgmanual/CG64510.htm

Entrepreneur's Relief

Entrepreneur's Relief is a capital gains tax reducer that few property investors can take advantage of as the relief does not apply to buy to lets or houses in multiple occupation.

The intention of the relief is to benefit business owners selling trading premises, but there is an opportunity for holiday let owners and letting agents trading from commercial premises they own to take advantage of a reduced rate of tax.

However, not all holiday lets meet the qualifying conditions:

- The property must be within the UK or EEA, not part of an overseas property business

See Page 63 for a list of EEA countries

- The property should be fully furnished an meet the availability and occupation rules for holiday lets

See Page 64 for full details of the qualifying rules for holiday lets

Limits and tax rates

Entrepreneur's Relief allows a property investor to pay capital gains tax at 10% on lifetime gains of up to £10 million on furnished holiday lets.

However, some clarification of the law is awaited as to whether the relief applies to part disposals of a holiday letting business.

HMRC is not keen to allow a property investor to claim the relief on selling one holiday let if they have a portfolio of several holiday letting properties.

Their argument is that the relief is intended to apply when a trading business is sold, not when individual parts of the business are disposed of.

If an owner has private use of a holiday let, Entrepreneur's Relief is apportioned to cover the business use of the premises only.

Action List

- ☑ Don't forget the tax traps that can exclude claiming PRR for part disposals of property
- ☑ Understand how PRR works and links in with Lettings Relief to cut capital gains tax bills - and keep detailed records of the periods owners have lived in a property to claim maximum relief
- ☑ Keep tenancy agreements as proof of dates a property you have lived in as your main home was let to track Lettings Relief
- ☑ If you have furnished holiday lets, check if Entrepreneur's Relief applies to your business

Chapter 14

Filling In Capital Gains Tax Returns

Chapter preview:

- Filling in a SA108 capital gains tax summary
- Claiming Foreign Tax Credit Relief
- Tips for dealing with estimated figures and foreign currency exchange rates

Completing a capital gains tax return is no more complicated than completing the property pages supplements of your Self-Assessment Tax Return.

In the previous two chapters, we've examined how to calculate capital gains tax and explained the formulas for working out part disposals, private residence relief and lettings relief.

This chapter explains how capital gains or losses are reported on special supplements to the Self-Assessment Tax Return just like rent and expenses for UK and overseas property businesses.

Worldwide gains for UK tax residents are reported on the SA108 capital gains summary and credit claimed against foreign tax paid are made on the SA106 foreign pages.

In simple terms, if you live in and pay taxes in the UK, it does not matter where the gain arises; you declare them all on the SA108, while tax relief on gains from property outside the UK are claimed by filing the SA106.

Filling In A SA108 Capital Gains Return

To complete this form, you must complete a computation for each gain or loss. If you dispose of more than one property other than your main home and/or other assets, such as stocks and shares, to which capital gains tax applies, attach a computation for each.

The form then becomes a summary or overview of your capital gains tax position for the year.

Download the form from Download the form: http://www.hmrc.gov.uk/forms/sa108.pdf

Your name - Your full name

Your Unique Taxpayer Reference (UTR) - This is a 10-digit number assigned by HM Revenue & Customs (HMRC). If you do not have a UTR, see Applying for a Unique Taxpayer Reference on Page 155.

Box 3 - Total gains - The figure in this box should equal the total of the sums in Boxes 21, 27, 33 and 34.

Importantly, enter the total amount of gains prior to deducting any losses, but after subtracting any reliefs, elections or claims except the annual exempt amount (AEA), which is deducted automatically by HMRC when the claim is received.

The AEA is deducted from the total gains for the year after completing this box.

For calculating capital gains tax, the AEA is often included in the template calculation for a single disposal, but should be left until this stage for multiple disposals.

Referring back to the capital gains tax worksheets in Chapter 12, for property investors, this is generally the net gain, less private residence relief and lettings relief

Special rules apply to deferred gains from before June 23, 2010 relating to Entrepreneurs' Relief. If you have these, speak to a professional tax adviser before filing your tax return.

Box 4 - Gains qualifying for Entrepreneurs' Relief (but ex-

cluding gains deferred from before 23 June 2010) - Enter the total gains from on or after April 6, 2013 and from between June 23, 2010 to April 5, 2011 that were deferred gains which qualified for Entrepreneurs' Relief.

Box 6 - Total losses for the year – Include all your allowable losses for the year.

Don't forget to keep a separate record for 'clogged losses'.

These are losses on disposals to connected persons, and losses from such disposals can only be offset against gains from other disposals to the same person.

Your calculation worksheets should also highlight any clogged losses and your relationship with the person to whom you made the disposal to in Box 37.

Do not include losses subject to Entrepreneurs' Relief in this box as they are accounted for in either Box 3 or 4.

Box 7 - Losses brought forward and used in the year - Enter a figure here if you have unused allowable losses brought forward from earlier tax years.

Again, if any clogged losses are included, put an explanation in Box 37.

Box 10 - Losses available to be carried forward to later years - This box is for totalling up any unused allowable losses for carrying forward to the next tax year, when they will be entered in Box 7.

Property, other assets and gains

Box 30 - Number of disposals - Put in the number of disposals of all assets subject to capital gains tax, and make sure the number tallies with the number of attached computations.

Box 31 - Disposal proceeds - Disposal proceeds are the amount of money you received for property, but if you sold at below market value, then the disposal proceeds for that transaction are taken as the open market value.

So, if you sold a property for £165,000 to an independent buyer, but sold a second one to a connected person for £100,000 when the open market value was £195,000, the disposal proceeds are £165,000 + £195,000 = £360,000.

Box 32 - Allowable costs (including purchase price) - Working from the template calculations in Chapter 12, this box contains the total of your property costs:

- Purchase prices
- Acquisition costs
- Disposal costs
- Improvement costs
- Costs of defending title to the property

Box 33 - Gains in the year, before losses - This is the total of property gains that go toward the total in Box 3, so follow the same guidance as for Box 3 above.

Box 34- Attributed gains where personal losses cannot be set off - Few taxpayers will need to complete this box – the figures only relate to trustees of a non-UK resident trust and the likelihood is a trustee or tax specialist will have provided these figures.

Box 35 - If you are making any claim or election - Put 'X' in this box if you are making a main residence election or claiming private residence relief and/or lettings relief.

Box 36 - If your computations include any estimates or valuations - Put 'X' in this box if you have included any estimated figures or are awaiting a surveyor's valuation of a property. Note the details in Box 37, including the date when you expect to have the final figures for amending the return.

Box 37 - Please give any other information in this space - This is for 'additional information'. Some examples of what you should put in to this box have already been pointed out above.

As a general rule, do not put too much detail in here beyond the minimum required to fully complete your tax return, as trying to be helpful will only trigger more questions from HMRC.

Claiming Foreign Tax Credit Relief

Tax regimes differ between countries and not all charge capital gains tax on the disposal of property.

However, if you do pay foreign tax on a property disposal, you should ask the tax authority which collected the tax to provide you with a certificate of tax paid.

All figures on this return should be in Sterling and any exchange rates should be based on HMRC's exchange rate tables.

Go to HMRC currency exchange rate tables – Link http://www.hmrc.gov.uk/exrate/index.htm

Box 33 – Amount of chargeable gain under UK rules – Calculate the gain on a disposal of the foreign property, including a furnished holiday let in the European Economic Area (EEA), according to UK capital gains tax rules.

Note that the box asks for the total net chargeable gain before deducting the AEA. Each disposal should have a separate calculation.

Boxes 34 to 36 – Ignore these as they are no longer used.

Box 37 – Foreign Tax Paid – This figure should be the same as the total for any certificates you have from foreign tax authorities.

Box 38 – Put an 'X' in the box to claim foreign tax credit relief. If this box is checked, providing you have enclosed the overseas tax certificates, capital gains calculations and filed the form on time, HMRC will work out any tax refund or payment due.

Box 39 – If you wish, you can work out your own foreign tax credit relief and enter the amount in this box.

Box 40 – Special Withholding Tax – This box only applies to taxpayers with undeclared gains under the UK/Switzerland Tax Co-Operation Agreement or where the disposal was made in another country charging a withholding tax.

Again the details should be on a certificate issued by the appropriate tax authority.

Action List

- ☑ Separate and record clogged losses relating to a connected person from other allowable losses
- ☑ Calculate all foreign gains and losses in Sterling according to HMRC's database of exchange rates
- ☑ Collect statements of account or other certificates for foreign tax withheld or paid to file with your UK tax return if you are claiming foreign tax credit relief
- ☑ Don't delay filing a tax return if some of the figures are not ready - estimate the figures, tell HMRC why you are using an estimate and give some idea of the date when the final figures will be available

Chapter 15

CGT Return Checklist

Chapter preview:

- Capital gains tax traps
- Disposal details
- Allowable expenses
- Part disposals
- Private residence relief
- Checking out valuations

This chapter takes you through another of HM Revenue & Customs (HMRC) tax toolkits highlighting common mistakes to be wary of.

This time, the checklist highlights issues tax inspectors look for in capital gains tax returns. The checklist is important for two reasons –

- HMRC will fine taxpayers for careless or deliberate errors on tax returns, so following their list of points to watch should reduce the chance of making mistakes
- Reverse engineering the checklist shows the points where tax inspectors focus for tax avoidance issues

Here, the main points of the capital gains tax property checklist are condensed for landlords and property investors.

For more detailed information, look at http://www.hmrc.gov.uk/agents/prereturn-support-agents.htm

The link includes a video on how to use the toolkits and links to downloads of full versions of each checklist.

Below, you can follow links for more in-depth reading on specific checklist points.

The toolkits relate to the SA 108 Capital Gains Tax Pages and SA106 Foreign Pages of the self-assessment tax return.

Capital Gains Tax Traps

1. The tax return is an aggregate sheet for the amounts included in all the capital gains tax computations for the year.

   Make sure the figures match the computation amounts and that all the computations for the tax year are included when the main tax return is filed.

   According to HMRC, 80% of capital gains tax returns are rejected because computations are not attached.

2. Do not deduct the annual exempt amount from your computations. HMRC does this automatically when working out your statement of account

3. Keep careful track of losses from previous years and make sure they are recorded and brought forward accurately.

4. Deduct allowable losses in the correct order.

   Start with losses from the same tax year as the gain – they are the losses that go in Box 6.

   Only deduct losses down to the annual exempt amount – you do not have to cancel out any more losses because the annual exempt amount does the job. In effect, you have your brought forward losses plus the annual exempt amount to set off against losses.

   Take the annual exempt amount away first, then the in-year losses, then the brought forward losses.

Any remaining losses are carried forward to the next tax year. The carry forward figure goes in Box 10.

As an example, you have made a gain of £60,000 and have in-year losses of £20,000, brought forward losses of £7,500 and an annual exempt amount of £11,000 for 2014-15.

The losses should be deducted like this:

	£	£
Chargeable gain for year		60,000
Annual exempt amount		(11,000)
Gross chargeable gain		49,000
Less		
Loss in year	(20,000)	
Loss brought forward	(7,500)	
		(27,500)
Add back annual exempt amount		11,000
Net chargeable gain		**32,500**

The annual exempt amount is deducted to show the amount of losses to offset and then added back to show the net chargeable gain.

HMRC will deduct the annual exempt amount automatically when the return is filed to adjust the total gain.

5. Don't forget to tick the estimated valuation boxes if the final valuation has not been received.

6. Check that Box 3 totals all chargeable gains for the year in Boxes 19, 25 and 31 before deducting

any reliefs, elections, claims or the annual exempt amount.

See Page 223

7. If the disposal is made overseas in a foreign currency, remember to convert the foreign currency value to Sterling using official HMRC exchange rates.

See Page 226

Disposal Details

1. Establish the correct date of disposal.

   For land and property the dates of acquisition and disposal are the dates when contracts were exchanged, not the completion dates.

See Page 188

2. If the sale proceeds are less than open market value, check that the market value of a property is included in the computation as disposal proceeds.

See Page 189

3. If a property valuation is needed, make sure one is completed before calculating any capital gains tax. HMRC will look for a valuation when land or property is:

   - Gifted but no cash changes hands
   - Sold to a connected person
   - A part disposal of a larger plot, such as a large garden
   - Is sold after acquisition before March 31, 1982
   - Inherited and disposed of

4. Give the surveyor a precise brief and make sure they are a member of the Royal Institution of Char-

tered Surveyors (RICS), not an estate agent.

The valuation should take account of:

- Does the property have a sitting tenant?
- Has refurbishment or an extension increased the value?
- Are any other assets included in the disposal?
- Was the property acquired before March 31, 1982?

Find a RICS surveyor - http://www.rics.org/uk/find-a-member/

5. Have all the beneficial owners with a financial interest in the disposal been identified?

   Everyone with a financial interest in a disposal should file a tax return with the proceeds and any expenses apportioned to their share of ownership.

   However, if the property is jointly owned and one owner is selling their share, only they need to file a capital gains tax return.

See Page 53 for more about beneficial ownership

Allowable expenses

1. Does the capital gains tax computation only include allowable expenses?

   Capital gains tax rules only allow specific expenses offset against disposal proceeds. Check any expenses in the computation to make sure they are allowed as capital costs.

See Chapter 12, Page 187

2. HMRC will look for a history of any improvements to a property and evidence that they are still present

at the time of disposal. If they are not, the expense cannot be claimed.

Do not include any improvement expenses incurred before March 31, 1982 as they should already be included in any valuation.

Part Disposals

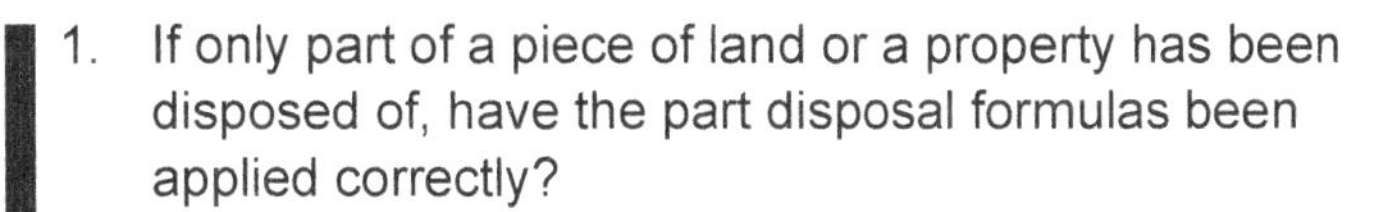

1. If only part of a piece of land or a property has been disposed of, have the part disposal formulas been applied correctly?

See Chapter 13, Page 204

2. If a part disposal computation has been filed in a previous tax year for the land or property, make sure that any apportioned allowable costs are properly calculated.

3. Check that the right acquisition cost is quoted for inherited properties.

See Chapter 12, page 192

Private Residence Relief

1. Private Residence relief is restricted if a property was not the only main residence throughout ownership.

   Tax inspectors will check to see if any nomination to elect a home as a main residence has been made by the beneficial owners or if main residence is a matter of fact.

See Chapter 13, Page 219 for more about main home elections

2. If the disposal relates to more than one building, does the computation reflect the correct amount of relief for any large grounds and gardens?

   The permitted area of land around a main home

must be a single plot and not several 'islands'. HMRC will want to identify the entire plot so that the correct reliefs can be applied to any gain.

See Chapter 13, Page 209 for more about grounds of more than 0.5 hectares

3. Where the garden and grounds including a main home are larger than the permitted area of 0.5 hectares, is relief available for the larger area?

   If the permitted area is larger than 0.5 hectares, private residence relief can only apply if the larger plot is needed for the owner's 'reasonable enjoyment' of the home.

   If the property covers several properties, then taxpayers can argue that the permitted area should be larger than 0.5 hectares.

See Chapter 13, Page 209

4. If main residence nomination has been made, private residence relief should only be applied to any gain on the nominated property.

   If a taxpayer has two homes, private residence relief can only be claimed against one.

   This home is either selected by written nomination or by proving which is the main home.

   Keep a record of nominations and dates to ensure any private residence relief claim is correctly calculated.

   Spouses and civil partners can have relief for one main home between them, so any nomination must be made jointly.

See Chapter 13, Page 219

5. Has any part of the property been used other than as a main home, such as for business or letting outside the Rent-A-Room scheme?

If so, private residence relief needs apportioning to the part of the property that was the main home.

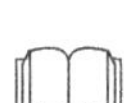

See Chapter 13, Page 205

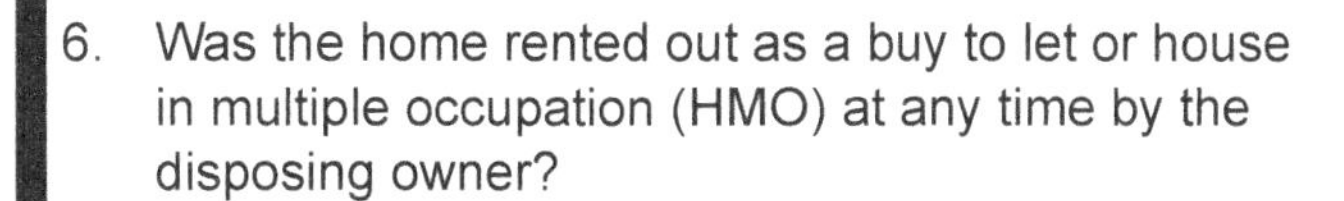

6. Was the home rented out as a buy to let or house in multiple occupation (HMO) at any time by the disposing owner?

   If so, private residence relief is restricted but lettings relief may apply.

See Chapter 13, Page 215

7. Was the home provided as the main residence for a dependent relative?

   This only applies if the relative moved in before April 5, 1988, and only one home per owner or joint owners can be subject of this relief.

   A dependent relative is:

   - A family member of the taxpayer or their spouse incapacitated by old age or illness
   - A relative of either of their mothers who is widowed, living apart from their husband or a single woman following the dissolution or annulment of a marriage

   Note the date limit on this relief.

Download the Capital Gains Tax for Land and Buildings Toolkit - http://www.hmrc.gov.uk/agents/toolkits/cgt-land-buildings.pdf

Checking out valuations

Consider a post transaction valuation check to agree the valuation of land or property with HMRC prior to submitting a capital gains tax return to confirm property values with the tax man and to avoid any unpleasant investigation.

See Chapter 14, Page 234

Action List

- ☑ Use this list to double check the points that trigger tax inquiries from HMRC on the SA108 Capital Gains Pages of your self-assessment tax return
- ☑ Remember not to deduct the annual exempt amount from any figures entered on the return - HMRC will do this automatically for you
- ☑ Don't forget to submit a copy of any computations and the workings to arrive at private residence relief or lettings relief with the tax return

Part IV

Special Property Tax Topics

Property tax is not only about income tax on rental profits and Capital Gains Tax - some special rules apply of which investors must be aware, otherwise they can easily fall into a tax trap. This part explains some of those rules for non-residents, new investors and householders who take in lodgers

Chapter 16

Getting A Grip On Stamp Duty

Chapter preview:

- Stamp duty rates and thresholds
- What stamp duty is charged on
- Unravelling chargeable considerations
- Watching out for linked transactions

Stamp duty rates and thresholds changed in Chancellor George Osborne's Autumn Statement 2014.

The regime was overhauled and the new rules have been in place for all property purchases completed after December 4, 2014.

The base threshold remains at 0% Stamp Duty Land Tax - stamp duty or SDLT for short - on residential land or property purchases up to £125,000.

The amount of stamp duty paid is based on working out the tax due on a 'chargeable consideration', which can vary depending on whether the property is:

- Residential or non-residential
- Freehold or leasehold
- Whether several transactions are linked

Some transactions are exempt from stamp duty or attract tax relief which lowers the tax due.

This chapter looks at the new stamp duty rules for residential land and property. Note that these rules apply to England and Wales. Scotland has separate rules which are not covered here.

For more about stamp duty in Scotland, go to the Revenue Scotland web site at https://www.revenue.scot/land-buildings-transaction-tax

Stamp Duty Rates And Thresholds

Stamp duty is charged as a percentage of the amount paid when property or land is bought or transferred, unless there is a relief or exemption.

Residential land or property stamp duty rates

Purchase price	Stamp Duty rate
Up to £125,000	0%
£125,001 to £250,000	2%
£250,001 to £925,000	5%
£925,001 to £1.5 million	10%
Over £1.5 million	12%

To calculate stamp duty, draw up a table with four columns and a row for each threshold up to the value of the property.

For example, Josh buys a home for £325,000. He calculates his stamp duty by splitting the value between the thresholds:

Threshold	Amount	Rate	Stamp duty
Up to £125,000	£125,000	0%	£0
£125,001 to £250,000	£125,000	2%	£2,500
£250,001 to £325,000	£75,000	5%	£3,750
TOTALS:	**£325,000**		**£6,250**

Companies pay stamp duty at 15% on homes costing more than £500,000.

The exception is that the stamp duty rates listed on the previous page apply when the home is used for a property rental business or for property development or trading.

What Stamp Duty Is Charged On

Stamp duty is paid when land or property is purchased or transferred, regardless of whether or not the transaction involves money or some other non-monetary payment, such as:

- Goods
- Services
- Assuming a person's financial liabilities or releasing them from debt
- Transferring an existing mortgage

The amount on which stamp duty is paid is called the 'chargeable consideration'.

A common scenario involving release from debt is when a couple who jointly own a house split up. One pays the other for their share of the equity and takes on the outstanding mortgage.

However, unless transferring mortgage debt is involved, stamp duty generally doesn't usually apply if the property is gifted without any chargeable consideration.

Unravelling Chargeable Considerations

Calculating the stamp duty payable on buying investment property is generally straightforward because the chargeable consideration is usually the purchase price.

The chargeable consideration does not include extras such as separate deals for carpets, curtains, furnishings or white goods.

Stamp duty is calculated on the value of the property including fixtures and fittings, not moveable goods.

However, sometimes, figuring out what is included in the chargeable consideration is more complicated. Besides the property and fixtures and fittings, some other factors need taking into account.

For example, if goodwill is part of the purchase of land or a building, this can attract stamp duty, as can the value of any estimate or agreement from the seller to repair the property - including any VAT due on the work or service.

Staged payments

If the seller agrees to split the payment for land or property, this does not delay paying stamp duty.

This 'postponed consideration' is a private deal and HM Revenue & Customs (HMRC) still expects full payment of stamp duty when the transaction completes.

For example, if the sale price is £800,000, but the seller agrees to accept £500,000 now and the balance 12 months later, stamp duty is charged on the full amount now.

This makes the bill £40,000 (£800,000 x 5%) on the date of completion.

Deferred payments

Conditional purchases which include an element of a sum of money down on completion and extra payment at a later date depending on a future event also attract special treatment.

HMRC will assume the future event will take place and base the value of the transaction on that basis. This is called a 'contingent consideration'.

A good example of such a deal would be a developer buying land on condition that an extra payment will be made should planning permission be granted.

If the builder paid £240,000 but agrees to pay another £100,000 if planning is granted, HMRC will agree to defer stamp duty on the £100,000, but will expect payment straight away on the £240,000.

The sting in the tail is that stamp duty on the £100,000 will not be zero because the amount is below the £125,000 threshold, but will be charged at 2% on £10,000 and 5% of £90,000 as the extra payment lifts the chargeable consideration up a threshold.

Uncertain payments

Sometimes the chargeable consideration is unknown for some reason - this is termed the 'uncertain consideration'. HMRC often views this as the problem with calculating stamp duty based on turnover, for example.

HMRC will look at a 'just and reasonable' estimate of value in these cases. If the estimate is too high when the value becomes more certain, taxpayers can appeal the payment.

Calculating Stamp Duty online

HMRC has put some calculators online to give some guidance in working out stamp duty transactions.

This link is for residential land and property purchases - http://www.hmrc.gov.uk/tools/sdlt/land-and-property.htm

This link is for calculating stamp duty on lease premiums - http://ldccalculator.hmrc.gov.uk/LDC01.aspx

Watching Out For Linked Transactions

If you are a property investors involved in a series of property transfers, then you need to watch out for linked transactions.

Linked transactions involve two or more properties but the same buyers and sellers, especially if they are 'connected persons'.

Failing to spot a linked transaction means the buyer must pay the stamp duty due on the total value of all the linked purchases.

This could be a disaster. Say an investor bought four properties worth £250,000 each from the same seller over a few months.

Instead of paying £5,000 stamp duty on each, calculated as 2% of £250,000, the total due is £100,000, worked out as 10% of £1 million.

If the properties are a mix of residential and non-residential land or property, then the non-residential stamp duty rate is applied to the total purchase amount.

When is a transaction 'linked'?

HMRC has three rules which make buying and selling land and property linked transactions:

- There are at least two transactions
- The same buyer and seller or people connected to either of them are involved in each transaction
- The transfers are a block sale or part of a series of transactions

Who are 'connected people'?

The list is the same as the list of connected people for capital gains tax.

Remember the relatives, spouses or civil partners of people on the list are also connected as well:

- Husbands, wives and civil partners
- Parents, grandparents and great-grandparents etc
- Brothers and sisters
- Children, grandchildren and great-children etc
- In-laws
- Business partners – but not joint property owners
- Any company you control or a person connected to you controls
- Any trust where you or a connected person are a beneficiary

Lineal descendants are always connected persons – so uncles, aunts, nephews, nieces and cousins are not included in the list but step-relatives are.

Single sale linked transactions

Even if a purchase is split and connected persons file separate paperwork for their part of the deal, the transaction can still be considered linked.

An example in HMRC guidance is that Mrs Smith buys a house and part of the garden, while her husband buys the rest of the garden as a separate building plot.

The transactions are linked as the buyers are connected and are purchasing from the same seller as a single deal.

In these cases, add up the total purchase prices to arrive at a single chargeable consideration.

Work out the stamp duty based on the aggregate purchase prices, then divide the amount between each buyer according to the purchase price they paid.

For example, if Mrs Smith paid £120,000 for the house and Mr Smith paid £80,000 for his land, the chargeable consideration is £200,000.

The stamp duty is £4,000 (£200,000 x 4%). Mrs Smith pays 12/20 (£2,400) and Mr Smith 8/20 (£1,600).

Had the couple treated the purchase as separate transactions, no stamp duty would be due as both paid under the £125,000 0% threshold.

Series linked transactions

The key to this rule is that no time limit applies to series linked transactions, so they are not always easy to spot and can come back to haunt property investors months or years after some of the purchases took place.

In some cases, buyers can end up owing more stamp duty on earlier purchases as later ones push them into a higher tax threshold.

Take this HMRC example of a property trader who has a deal with a builder. The trader buys three houses from a builder over a couple of years.

The purchases are connected because the same buyer and seller are involved.

The buyer pays £180,000 for each house when building finishes.

To calculate the stamp duty, work out the amount due on the total chargeable consideration for all the transactions to date at the rates in force at the time of that transaction.

Then divide this amount between each transaction pro rata to the value as a share of the total chargeable consideration.

Here's the example worked through:

Transaction 1: Tax is due on £180,000 as:

- 0% on £125,000
- 2% on £55,000
- Total stamp duty: £1,100.

Transaction 2: Tax due on the total consideration of £360,000 is:

- 0% on £125,000
- 2% on £125,000
- 5% on £110,000
- Total stamp duty: £8,000.

At this stage the tax due on each transaction is £4,000, so an additional £2,900 is due for the first transaction.

Transaction 3: Tax due on the total consideration of £540,000 is:

- 0% on £125,000
- 2% on £125,000
- 5% on £290,000

> - Total £17,000.
>
> At the end of the linked transaction, stamp duty on each transaction is £5,666, so an extra £1,666 is required to pay for the first and second transactions.

If the transactions were not linked, the stamp duty payable on the second and third transactions would have been the same as on the first, making a total of £3,300.

Action List

☑ Check out stamp duty rates and thresholds before making a purchase to see if you can't save money by agreeing a slightly lower purchase price

☑ Stamp duty can be complicated - read the rules on linked transactions and connected persons to avoid a surprise bill

☑ Residential and non-residential property have different rates - don't apply the wrong rate or your calculations will be incorrect

For non-residential stamp duty rates and thresholds, go to https://www.gov.uk/government/publications/rates-and-allowances-stamp-duty-land-tax/rates-and-allowances-stamp-duty-land-tax

Only residential stamp duty rates and thresholds changed on December 4, 2014 - the rest remained unchanged

Chapter 17

Rent-A-Room Tax Relief

Chapter preview:

- Rent less than £4,250 a year
- Rent more than £4,250 a year
- Reducing Rent-A-Room relief
- Rent-A-Room losses
- Changing circumstances

Rent-A-Room relief can come in two types – either letting a furnished room in your home to a single lodger or sharing a house in multiple occupation (HMO) that you manage with several other tenants.

Rent-A-Room relief allows you to earn up to £4,250 a year tax free – or £2,125 each if you are a couple letting a room.

The bonus is you do not have to account for the money on a tax return providing you stick to the rules.

The key points to keep in mind are:

- The letting room must be furnished residential space, not space let for business, such as an office or storage
- You must live in the property – but the home can be a static caravan or houseboat as well as a flat or house
- You can own or rent – but if you rent or live in a lease-

hold home you must have permission to sub-let from the landlord and any mortgage lender

- Check your home insurance. Standard home insurance policies do not cover letting to lodgers and you may have to take out a special policy

- By default, Rent-A-Room applies to individual householders and not companies or partnerships

- You don't have to pay tax to take advantage of Rent-A-Room relief, so it's an ideal income boost for students, the unemployed or pensioners

Rent Less Than £4,250 A Year

If you are paid £4,250 a year - £81 a week - or less by lodgers, you have no tax to pay but cannot set off any expenses or losses against tax either.

For Rent-A-Room, a 'year' means the tax year of April 6 to the following April 5.

That £4,250 does not have to be from the same lodger, so if you take in two or three during the year, keep an eye on how much you are earning in total to stay below the tax threshold.

If you have expensive repairs in mind, think about coming out of Rent-A-Room for that year and including the income from a lodger with the rest of your property income.

That way you can offset the cost of repairs and losses against other rental income and then dip back into the Rent-A-Room scheme in the next year.

To do this, you must make an election. This means not putting an 'X' in Box 4 of the UK Property Pages and including the income in your total rents in Box 20 on page two.

The election must be received by HM Revenue & Customs (HMRC) within 12 months of the January 31following the end of the tax year you want your Rent-A-Room income treated as buy to let income.

To simplify the dates, that means if you want your 2014-15 Rent-

A-Room income tax treated as other letting income, your tax year ends on April 5, 2015 and you must make your election to HMRC by January 31, 2017.

To elect to switch back into the Rent-A-Room scheme, put an 'X' in Box 4.

Rent More Than £4,250 A Year

If your Rent-A-Room income is more than £4,250, then your rental income and expenses are automatically treated like any other rental income for tax purposes.

However, you can elect to be taxed on the difference between the total rents received from lodgers and the £4,250 Rent-A-Room threshold.

This is how the election works:

Alyssa lets two rooms in her home to lodgers for £70 a week each, which adds up to £7,280 a year.

She has letting expenses of £1,700, so makes a profit of £5,580 on which she pays tax at the basic rate (20%) of £1,116.

However, if she elects to pay tax on the profit over the Rent-A-Room threshold, she only pays income tax on £7,280 – £4,250, which is £3,030. Her tax then reduces to £606, but she makes no claim for the letting expenses while still saving £510 tax.

To make the election, leave Box 4 blank and put £4,250 in Box 37.

Reducing Rent-A-Room Relief

The Rent-A-Room limit of £4,250 is reduced 50% to £2,125 if another householder in the same property received letting income from lodgers in the home.

For instance, the home may be shared by two or more householders who let to a lodger jointly.

If the let is less than 12 months, the £4,250 limit reduces to £2,125 if another householder lets furnished residential accommodation in the same home at any time in the tax year.

A quirk is Rent-A-Room legislation allows the £2,125 relief to three other householders.

Here's an HMRC example from the Property Income Manual produced as guidance for tax inspectors:

Sisters Judy, Pat and Josephine own and occupy Sandy View during the year ended April 5, 2014.

Each lets one room to a lodger.

Pat is a qualifying individual as Sandy View is her main home, but Josephine and Judy live elsewhere.

In calculating Pat's Rent-A-Room limit the basic amount is divided by two - not by three -because at the same time Sandy View was Pat's main residence Josephine and Judy were letting rooms in the same property. So, Pat's limit is halved to £2,125.

If Josephine and Judy had also been qualifying individuals their limit would have been £2,125 each. The fact that total exemptions or deductions in that case might have extended to £6,375 (3 x £2,125) is irrelevant.

Rent-A-Room Losses

Losses cannot be generated under the Rent-A-Room scheme, but if a landlord expects to spend more than £4,250 on business expenses in a tax year, they should consider an election to have the letting income dealt with under normal profit and loss rules.

Any Rent-A-Room loss can then be offset against other rental income. Once the losses are wiped off the accounts, switch back to the Rent-A-Room scheme.

This is done by making an election as described above.

Changing Circumstances

Rent-A-Room relief is not available where the property ceased to be the taxpayer's main home before the letting began, even if the letting started in the same tax year.

The householder's circumstances may change during the Rent-A-Room period, and if they do, a whole host of special rules can apply.

Here, we look at some common issues that can arise:

Letting more than one room

A householder can let out any number of furnished rooms in their home, but the Rent-A-Room threshold does not apply to separate properties, rooms or tenants but to a taxpayer, so remains £4,250 a year.

Another point to be aware of is house in multiple occupation (HMO) licensing in some neighbourhoods.

Many councils define a small HMO as a home where three unrelated tenants share cooking and washing facilities. These properties may need licensing, so check HMO rules with your local council before taking in a tenant.

Landlord has more than one home

It's a tax rule that a person can only have one main home at a time, and for capital gains tax, this is normally dealt with by a main home election.

However, an unmarried couple living together may well each have a main home.

HMRC will object to claims for Rent-A-Room relating to two different main homes for the same tax year and will determine which property is really the taxpayers main home by looking at where friends and official correspondents would expect to contact them.

An important point to remember is the property where the lodger lives must be the householder's main home for some of the lodger's period in residence, but not the whole time.

See Page 217 for more about main home elections

Landlord moves home

If the landlord moves home and lets to the same or a different a lodger under Rent-A-Room, treat the rents from each property as a combined Rent-A-Room income.

Then, look at the sections above relating to rents above and below £4,250 a year and see which tax computation suits your financial circumstances best and make the appropriate election on your tax return.

Moving overseas or getting a home with a job

An expat landlord letting out their UK home while overseas does not qualify for Rent-A-Room relief because wherever they are living becomes their main home.

Similarly, if a householder takes up a job with accommodation, that becomes their main home regardless of if the new home is whether the UK or overseas.

In both of these examples, Rent-A-Room continues until the end of the tax year in which the householder moves and then ceases.

Landlord moves leaving lodger behind

Sometimes breaking up is hard to do, so if a householder with a lodger moves to a new home leaving the former home unsold and the lodger still in occupation, rent from the letting qualifies for Rent-A-Room relief until the end of the tax year during which the householder moved.

HMRC does not care whether the lodger has use of all or just part of the home.

Action List

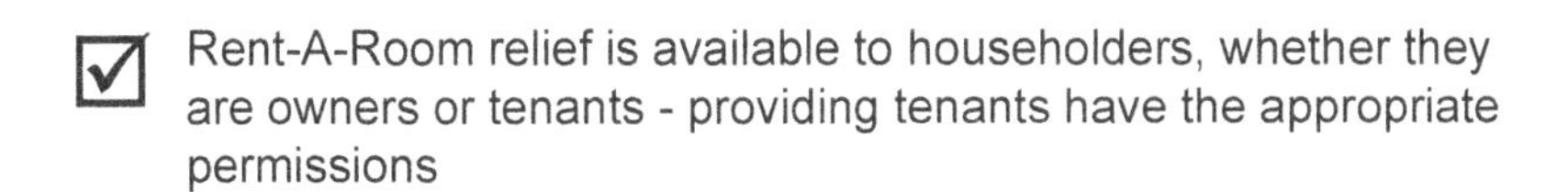
Rent-A-Room relief is available to householders, whether they are owners or tenants - providing tenants have the appropriate permissions

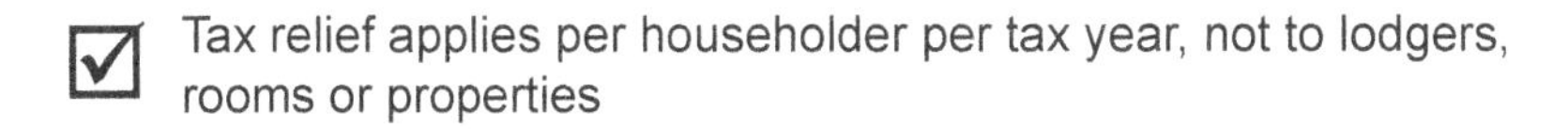
Tax relief applies per householder per tax year, not to lodgers, rooms or properties

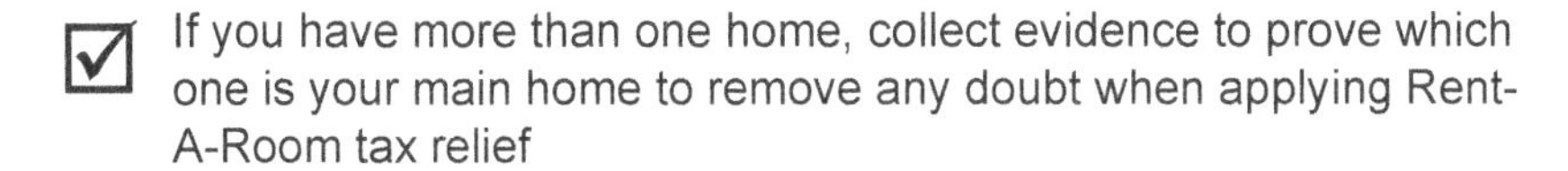
If you have more than one home, collect evidence to prove which one is your main home to remove any doubt when applying Rent-A-Room tax relief

Chapter 18

Tax For Property Traders

Chapter preview:

- Tax for buy to sell traders
- Trading stock and work-in-progress
- Business expenses for property traders
- Keeping financial records for property traders

In earlier chapters, we looked at the difference between property investing and property trading or development.

For tax, someone who owns property is either an investor or a trader – the popular term 'developer' can apply to either and is not recognised under tax legislation.

In this chapter, we look at the fine, grey line between investing and trading and some of the tax differences that have to be considered.

Many property people believe they run a single business regardless of the nature of their activities. As we saw in Chapter 3, this is incorrect.

Property trading is a separate business from letting and is treated for tax as any other trading business, for example as a shop, garage or online retailer.

The principle is straightforward. In earlier chapters, we looked at the difference between property investing and property trading or development.

Investors often classify themselves as landlords, developers or traders.

A property trader is a speculator who buys and holds property as stock.

In most cases, value is added to the stock by refurbishment and the stock is then sold as soon as possible for a profit.

Tax For Buy To Sell Traders

Property traders pay income tax on their profits – no capital gains tax is payable on the buying and selling of property stock in a trading business.

Any incidental letting income is pooled with any holiday let or investment property income and reported on the UK property pages of a tax return.

Letting a trading property does not change the business status from trading to a UK property business.

A property bought to trade will always remain a trading property and have income tax charged against any profits, while a letting property will always be part of a UK property business and have income tax charged against rental profits and capital gains tax against any appreciation in value.

Determining trading status is important for property people need to apply the correct tax treatment to each property transaction.

As income tax is charged on profits, a single house sale is likely to push a trader into the higher rate (40%) tax bracket each year.

For part-time traders who may have a salary or other income, this could be a tax disaster.

For this reason, most traders form a limited company to buy and hold their trading property. With a limited company, corporation tax is paid on profits at 20%, but no more tax is due for basic rate taxpayers on dividends.

Higher rate taxpayers can keep the profits within the company and draw them down as and when they are needed. This way, higher rate taxpayers can manipulate the tax they pay each year.

A rule of thumb for tax is that if you can't avoid it, defer it, and that's exactly what trading within a limited company does.

If you do let a trading property, the rental income is declared on the UK property business pages, but the subsequent sale will go through the accounts as a trade.

For more about property companies, see Chapter 20

Trading Stock And Work-In-Progress

One of the key differences between investment and trading is that buy to let homes are assets generating income while buy to sell homes are stock generating trading profits.

HM Revenue & Customs (HMRC) taxes income from investments differently to income from a trade.

As properties in a trading business are treated as stock, any money spent on adding value to them is 'held' on the accounts and not offset against profits until the property is sold.

Holding stock and adding value with ongoing refurbishment or work-in-progress (WIP) are not the same as landlords carrying out repairs and improvements.

Here's a worked example to show how this applies to a property trader:

In January 2015, Mike buys a doer-upper for £275,000 plus legal fees and stamp duty of £3,750. Prior to the purchase in December, Mike also had a survey carried out for which he paid £375.

In February 2015, Mike gained planning permission for an extension and had an architect draft some drawings. This cost £15,000.

By June, the extension and other works on the property were completed, costing £45,000.

The property was then sold for £395,000 in September 2015.

The stock account for the property looks like this in Mike's books:

Date	Item	DR	CR
Dec 2014	Valuation	£375	
Jan 2015	Property purchase	£275,000	
	Stamp duty and fees	£3,750	
Feb 2015	Planning	£15,000	
Jun 2015	Building works	£45,000	
Sep 2015	Sale price		£395,000
	Legal fees	£650	
	Profit/(Loss)	£55,255	
	Totals:	**£395,000**	**£395,000**

Although Mike spent cash on buying and adding value to the property, he cannot offset that expenditure against other profits until the property is sold.

If he were a sole trader, he would be liable to pay income tax and national insurance on the entire £55,255 earned in the tax year, pushing him into the 40% tax bracket before adding any other income.

Had he formed a property trading company, the company would have paid corporation tax at 20% (£11,051), leaving £44,204 in the bank for reinvestment or to draw as dividends.

For joint venture property deals, traders often form companies called 'SPVs' or 'special purpose vehicles'. These companies have shareholdings allocated on incorporation for the division of any expected profits.

Other trading stock accounting issues come into play for house builders regarding valuing stock held on the books, for example when the business owns multiple properties.

If you intend to embark on a career as a property trader, consult an appropriately experienced and qualified accountant who can steer you through a minefield of potential problems.

Business Expenses For Property Traders

As we have seen above, refurbishment costs are split from general business expenses for traders.

This allows traders to charge day-to-day business expenses against profits in the same way as landlords. These general expenses would be office costs, transport, tools and business insurance etc.

One notable difference between the expenses a trader may claim which an investor can't are the costs of property purchases that fall through.

Investors cannot claim for surveys, legal costs or any other related travel or advertising expenses but traders can.

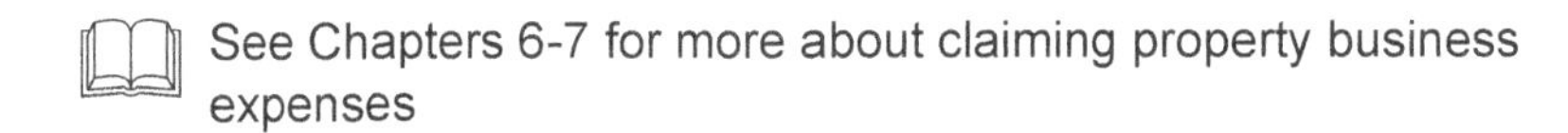
See Chapters 6-7 for more about claiming property business expenses

Keeping Financial Records For Traders

It's important for property people running investment and trading businesses at the same time to keep the financial records for each business separate.

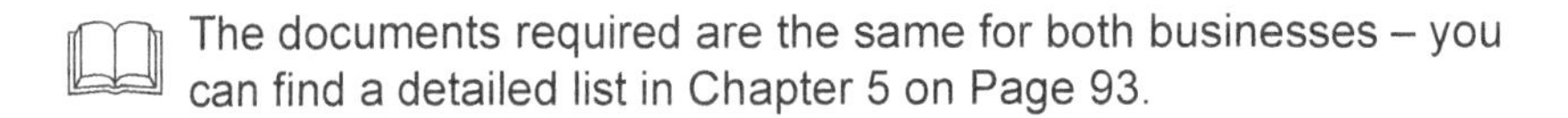
The documents required are the same for both businesses – you can find a detailed list in Chapter 5 on Page 93.

Remember that the list for capital gains tax applies to property traders – but income tax applies instead of capital gains tax.

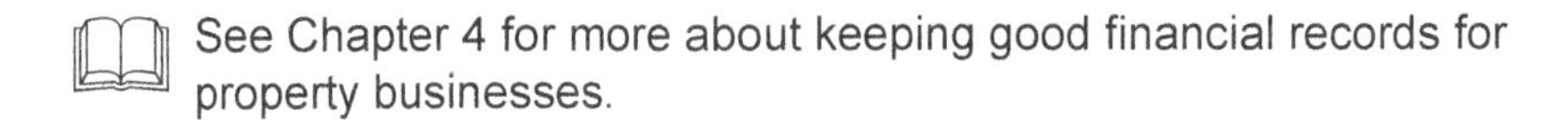
See Chapter 4 for more about keeping good financial records for property businesses.

Action List

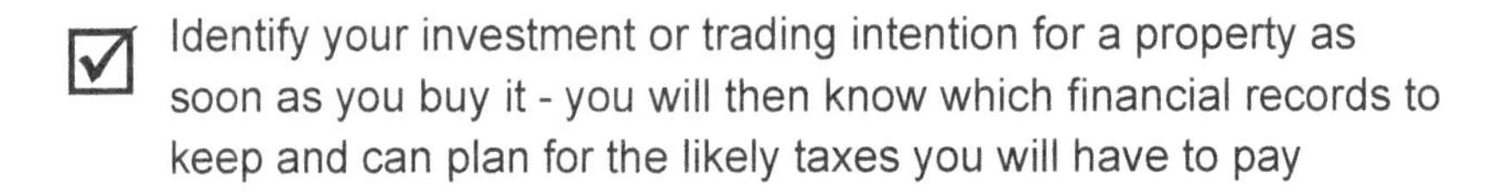
☑ Identify your investment or trading intention for a property as soon as you buy it - you will then know which financial records to keep and can plan for the likely taxes you will have to pay

☑ Run the figures for personal v corporate ownership of trading property

Chapter 19

Non-Resident Landlord Tax

Chapter preview:

- Tax options for non-resident landlords
- What is a usual place of abode'?
- The Non-Resident Landlord Scheme (NRLS)
- Joining NRLS

Landlords who live outside the United Kingdom but have land or property here come under some special tax rules.

These rules can apply to former UK taxpayers who now live abroad but still have property in Britain, or foreign property investors who own property in the United Kingdom but have never lived here.

The rules for both are tricky, with some tax pitfalls along the way while a whole new set of capital gains tax rules for non-residents are due to start on April 5, 2015.

This chapter looks at income tax on rents for property owners who are tax resdient outside the UK..

This information is provided as a starting point for looking at cross-border property tax issues. If you are a non-resident landlord or investor with land or property in the UK, you really need expert advice from a tax professional in each country you have property and in the place you call home.

Besides tax on rents and property disposals, you need to know about estate planning and inheritance tax in each country and how this may affect your last wishes.

For more information about the new capital gains tax rules, go to Chapter 13 Special CGT Rules For Landlords

Tax Options For Non-Resident Landlords

HM Revenue & Customs (HMRC) runs the Non-Resident Landlord Scheme (NRLS) so tenants and letting agents in the UK can pay income tax due on rents for landlords living overseas.

Short-term trips abroad do not qualify – so spending a few weeks or months abroad does not mean you become a non-resident landlord.

The cut-off point is six months.

Any landlord with a 'usual place of abode' overseas for six months or more in a tax year has two options:

- Join the Non-Resident Landlord Scheme so tenants and letting agents can withhold tax due on rents paid
- Apply to receive rents without any withheld tax deducted and report rental income and expenses on a self-assessment tax return, providing:
    - They have kept their UK tax affairs up to date
    - No tax is owed in the UK
    - They do not expect to pay income tax in the UK
    - They agree to file self-assessment tax returns each year

What Is A 'Usual Place Of Abode'?

A 'usual place of abode' is not the same as tax residence, but the place where the non-resident landlord spends most of their time. A non-resident landlord can even be tax resident in the UK, even though they generally live outside the country.

For example, they may come to the UK for a few months to care for a sick relative or for a long visit yet keep a home overseas.

Companies incorporated outside the UK are generally treated as having a usual abode outside the UK, unless for some reason they are treated for tax purposes as resident.

The Non-Resident Landlord Scheme

The Non-Resident Landlord Scheme (NRLS) is the HMRC process for collecting any tax due on rental profits on property owned by landlords living overseas.

The tax is paid by either a letting agent or the tenant.

If the landlord is a joint owner and the other joint owners are UK resident, tax is only paid on their own share of rental income generated by the property.

De minimis limits

Tenants who pay rent of less than £100 a week to non-resident landlords do not have to withhold and account for income tax unless they have been told to do so by HMRC.

Letting agents do not have a de minimis limit.

Unless HMRC notifies them in writing not to withhold tax on rents, they must do so, but they can deduct any property business expenses to arrive at a net rent before doing so.

Tenants and NRLS

If a landlord lives overseas and £100 a week or more rent is paid, they must register with HMRC and deduct tax from the rent before paying the balance to the landlord.

Tenants should also register with HMRC if they pay someone who is not a letting agent on behalf of a landlord, such as a friend or relative.

They don't need to deduct tax if HMRC told them in writing that they can pay the landlord without withholding tax, but they still must register with HMRC and file an annual financial report.

Letting agents and NRLS

Letting agents must withhold tax on rents collected unless HMRC has told them otherwise in writing.

A letting agent for NRLS is someone who:

- Runs a UK property business for an overseas landlord
- Is paid or controls how rent is paid for an overseas landlord
- Lives in the UK for more than six months a year

A letting agent includes estate agents, solicitors, accountants, friends or relatives.

Tenant-finders and NRLS tax

If you find tenants for overseas landlords you don't have to withhold tax under NRLS if:

- You collect your fees sourcing tenants direct from rental payments

  And

- Rent is collected for no more than three months and the tax due is £100 or less

For example, Derek finds a tenant for a property rented at £600 per month.

He collects the rent for two months to reimburse his fee and to pay his expenses. The tenant then pays the rent direct to the landlord.

After Derek has deducted his fee and expenses of £800, the tax due is £80 so the transaction falls outside the NRLS.

However, if Derek sourced a tenant for a home rented out for £8,000 a year and collected rent for six months to pay his fees and expenses plus insurance and to fund some repairs, even if the tax due was £100 or less, he would have to operate NRLS because he collected the rent for more than three months.

Joining NRLS

If you are a non-resident landlord and want to have your rents paid direct without a tenant or letting agent withholding tax you can join the Non-Resident Landlord Scheme.

However, you must register with HMRC within 30 days of the start of a tenancy or report any existing tenancies by completing HM Revenue & Customs Form NRL1i.

Download Form NRL1i: https://www.gov.uk/government/publications/non-resident-landlord-application-to-receive-uk-rental-income-without-deduction-of-uk-tax-individuals-nrl1i

Letting agents should use form NRL4i, which is also available on the link above.

Tenants should write to HMRC with their name and address and details of the landlord, stating a wish to register for NRLS.

Tax should be paid to HMRC within 30 days of the end of each tax quarter - on June 30, September 30, December 31 and March 31.

Anyone deducting tax on rents at source should send a report to HMRC using form NRLY and a certificate of tax paid to the landlord on a form NRL6 each year by July 5.

Download a Form NRLY: https://www.gov.uk/government/publications/non-resident-landlord-annual-information-return-nrly

Download a Form NRL6: https://www.gov.uk/government/publications/non-resident-certificate-of-tax-liability-to-be-provided-to-non-resident-landlords-by-uk-letting-agents-or-tenants-nrl6

The tax records should be kept for four years and should include:

- Dates and amounts of rent you've received by letting agents or paid, if you're a tenant
- Any correspondence with the landlord
- Dates, a brief description, receipts and amounts of any expenses paid for the landlord

Working out NRLS withholding tax

These calculations should be run every tax quarter:

- Add up the gross rent due in the past three months
- Deduct any allowable business expenses paid in the quarter to give the net rent
- Multiply the net rent by the basic rate of income tax – currently 20%

HMRC will check that the right amount is paid and may charge interest on late payments.

Here's an example of how to work out the tax due:

Jenny is a tenant with an overseas landlord who paid £2,250 rent between June 30 and September 30, 2014. She accounted for the money as follows:

- £350 for plumbing repairs paid by the letting agent
- £100 for servicing a boiler
- £1,800 paid direct to the landlord

Because the plumbing and boiler repairs are allowable expenses, they are excluded from the tax calculation.

The tax is paid on £1,800 at the basic rate of 20% - so, a payment of £360 is due to HMRC.

Julie can deduct this money from her rent or other money owed to the landlord.

Action List

Run the figures and work out which tax option suits you best while living overseas

HMRC has some flexibility about time limits for expat landlords, but if you do not have written permission, your tenant or letting agent must deduct income tax at source at the basic rate

Chapter 20

Owning Property With A Company

Chapter preview:

- You are not your company
- Owning property with a company
- How company income is taxed
- How companies shield tax on rents
- Extra corporate benefits
- Deciding if a company is for you

One of the common questions property investors ask is whether they should put their properties into a company or own them personally.

The answer is tricky because the best option for one investor may not sit right with another.

Something which confuses the issue is that the answer can change according to who is sitting in 10 Downing Street and their attitude towards taxing businesses.

The general rule of thumb is companies are good for mitigating personal tax but not so good at holding assets, while the 20% tax band clouds the issue as well.

The basic rate of tax for an individual is 20% and so is the basic rate of Corporation Tax for companies with annual profits of £300,000 or less.

This means many property investors can pay less income tax

on rental profits that are made through a company than they do as individuals under the higher rate (40%) or top rate (45%) tax bands.

Sharp-eyed investors will also note that companies do not pay capital gains tax but rather corporation tax on chargeable gains when disposing of a property. As higher rate and above taxpayers pay capital gains tax at 28%, this and other corporate chargeable gains benefits can look inviting as well.

To emphasise, whenever a discrepancy between tax rates arises, the door opens on an opportunity for saving tax.

The discussion about investing as a property company is lengthy and complex and falls outside the scope of this book. It's certainly worth us sketching an outline, but anyone contemplating trading as a property investment company should discuss the matter with a tax professional before making changes to the way they do business.

You Are Not Your Company

In British law, a company is a separate legal entity and pays tax, owns property and conducts financial affairs in its own name.

The company is owned by the shareholders, who may or may not be directors, and who are paid a share of the profits the company makes as a dividend.

Directors make the day-to-day business decisions as officers of the company and have legal responsibilities to file accounts, tax returns and other official documents.

Dividends are paid pro rata according to the number of shares someone owns, so if the company wants to pay out £10,000 profits, and three shareholders own 250, 200 and 50 shares each, the profits are split.

- A with 250 shares is paid £5,000 (50% of the profit)
- B with 200 shares is paid £4,000 (40% of the profit)
- C with 50 shares is paid £1,000 (10% of the profit)

Income shifting by reallocating the shareholding is a real

advantage for joint owners. Income shifting within a company means altering the number of shares held by basic and higher rate taxpayers so those who pay income tax at the lowest rate are paid more of the profits.

As you will see, this allows basic rate taxpayers to draw down company profits without paying any additional tax.

A company is like a financial battery storing up money instead of electricity.

This income can be shielded within a company for an almost indefinite time. For example, the directors decide when dividends are paid, so profits can be held by the company during times when the shareholders are working in other jobs and earning a salary that puts them in a high tax bracket.

When those shareholders see their earnings decrease or they retire, the company can then pay out those stored up dividends as a lump sum or drip feed them over several tax years.

This way, shareholders can minimise the tax they pay, and if they are canny, keep their income tax below the higher tax rates.

Individuals do not have that option. They must pay their income tax and capital gains tax as it falls due, so if they make big profits in one year that pushes them up into high rate tax brackets, they just have to pat the tax due.

Remember company shareholdings can be adjusted at any time and the Form 17 procedure for individuals does not apply.

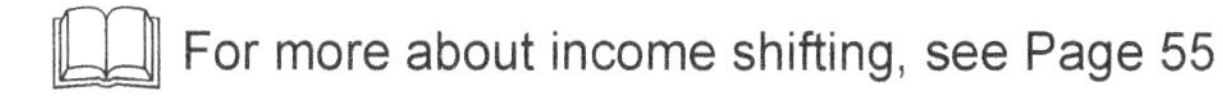
For more about income shifting, see Page 55

Owning Property With A Company

This mainly involves buy to let investment property, not so much furnished holiday lets or other business premises.

Generally, many businesses can form a company and transfer property and other assets into it without paying capital gains tax on the switch by applying for incorporation relief.

However, this option is not open to landlords because their

business is not considered a trade but an investment.

As incorporation relief is not an option, the cost of switching property you already own into a company is prohibitive as capital gains tax and stamp duty will be charged.

Effectively, an investor is selling the property to the company and the normal transaction charges between a buyer and seller apply.

A typical workaround is to leave properties owned before incorporation in their current state of ownership and to buy any new investment properties through the company.

Furnished holiday lets and the premises where your property business trades generally have incorporation relief if they switch from private to corporate ownership.

How Company Income Is Taxed

Companies pay corporation tax instead of income tax and capital gains tax.

Property investors should be aware of some important differences between the way companies and individuals tax some income and expenses.

The rate of corporation tax depends on the annual profits returned by a company.

Profits up to £300,000 are taxed at a rate of 20%. Higher profits attract increased tax rates.

The good news is associated company rules disappear in April 2015, which means property investors with wider business interests can consider corporate buy to let ownership.

Current low corporation tax rates are the main reason property people are looking at running their businesses as a company.

However, corporation tax rates have not always been so low and are subject to change when Chancellors announce their Budgets.

With long-term investment planning, no one can be sure that today's rates will still be in place in a decade or so down the line.

Dividend tax rates

Once profits are drawn as dividends, individuals pay income tax on their earnings at a rate based on their overall annual income.

A basic rate taxpayer can earn up to £41,865 before paying higher rate tax at 40%.

The £41,865 is made up from the £31,865 you can earn at basic rate tax and your £10,000 personal allowance.

Not everyone has a £10,000 personal allowance, so before considering income shifting, check your allowance with HM Revenue & Customs (HMRC).

Income tax is paid at these rates for the 2014-2015 tax year:

Dividend income	Tax rate after deducting personal allowances
<= £31,865	10%
£31,866 60 £150,000	32.5%
£150,001 +	37.5%

How dividends are paid

Companies may have thousands of shareholders and monitoring the personal tax for each would be impossible.

Instead, a dividend voucher is issued to each shareholder showing:

- The dividend paid
- The tax credit against that payment at the basic rate

If the shareholder is a basic rate taxpayer, then no more tax is due, but higher rate taxpayers will have to pay more.

Understanding dividend tax credits

As a company has already paid corporation tax on profits, shareholders receive a tax credit against their dividends so the same money is not taxed twice.

The dividend paid is 90% of the declared 'dividend income', while the other 10% is the tax credit, so, a shareholder receiving a £5,000 dividend picks up £4,500 dividend income and a £500 tax credit.

- If you pay basic rate income tax:

  No more tax is due on your dividend income because the tax liability of 10% equals the tax credit

- If you pay tax at the higher rate:

  You pay an extra 32.5% tax on dividend income by declaring the income on your self-assessment tax return

Note, you cannot claim the 10% tax credit if you do not pay income tax because the 10% is a credit against tax due.

If you pay no income tax you have nothing against which to credit the payment.

How Companies Shield Tax On Rents

The best way to explain how companies can shield tax on rents is with an example.

Martin is a higher rate taxpayer (40%) with rental profits of £9,000 a year as a director of a company that owns several buy to let homes.

If he paid income tax on those profits, he would be charged at 40% and has to pay HMRC £3,600, leaving him with £5,400.

However, because the company owns the properties and assuming total profits subject to corporation tax are less than £300,000 and no associated companies are involved, the company pays tax at 20%, which is £1,800 and leaves the company with £7,200.

Martin can decide to leave the money in the company until he pays income tax at a lower rate or draw some or all of the cash as a dividend.

If he was a lower rate taxpayer, he could draw money as a dividend and pay no extra tax. This is one reason why many landlords collect cash in a company as retirement savings, as a company can hold the profits until they become lower rate taxpayers.

Companies And Chargeable Gains

Companies do not pay capital gains tax, but they still have to pay tax on chargeable gains in the same way as individuals.

Any capital gains from the disposal of property are added to the company's profits and charged to corporation tax.

A company has no annual exempt amount and cannot claim personal reliefs like principle residence relief (PRR) or lettings relief as an individual can.

However, a company can claim indexation relief which takes the sting of inflation out of a capital gain and is a tax reducer.

A company can also claim capital costs in the same way as an individual property owner, such as the purchase price, acquisition costs, improvements, sale costs and any costs of defending the property title.

Calculating indexation relief

HMRC has published an indexation factor every month since March 1982. The indexation factor reflects any changes in the Retail Price Index.

Indexation relief is calculated by multiplying the purchase price or open market value of the property on the date the property took over ownership of the home by the factor for that month.

The formula is:

Purchase cost x Indexation factor for month of acquisition = Indexation relief

For example, ABC Properties Ltd bought a buy to let home for £100,000 in March 2001. The property was sold in September 2014 for £230,000 and had rental profits of £12,500 in the year. The indexation factor for March 2001 is 0.496.

Using the formula:

£100,000 x 0.496 = Indexation relief of £49,600

This reduces the chargeable gain for the company to:

£100,000 - £49,600 = £50,400

Company income subject to corporation tax is:

£50,400 + £12,500 = £62,900

Bear in mind two rules about corporate gains:

- Companies can only offset indexation relief pound for pound as a tax reducer against a chargeable gain. If the relief comes to more than the gain, then the excess is lost.

- If a property was acquired by a company before March 1982, then the purchase cost is the higher of the actual purchase price or an open market valuation of the property on March 31, 1982.

Download HMRC Indexation Relief Tables - https://www.gov.uk/government/uploads/system/uploads/attachment_data/file/367779/sept14-ct-cgains.pdf

Extra Corporate Benefits

For some landlords, personal reasons rather than tax benefits may make owning property with a company an attractive option.

Limited liability and extending ownership to more than four investors are important aspects here.

Limited liability

Limited liability is a shield protecting directors and shareholders from personal financial exposure if the property business fails.

Providing a company is run honestly, should it go into liquidation or stop trading, creditors can only demand that the shareholders pay compensation up to the value of their equity stake.

Unlike sole or joint property owners who face a call on their personal assets, like their homes, investments and other assets if their business fails, directors and shareholders are protected by the shield of limited liability.

Banks and other organisations will try to subvert limited liability by asking for personal guarantees.

A personal guarantee is a director signing away limited liability protection offered by the company to allow a creditor to seize their personal assets if the company fails.

This is not something that a director should agree to lightly as a personal guarantee undermines one of the main advantages of trading as a company.

Another liability issue is buying property with a company trading in another sector, for example a business consultant trading as a company may buy investment property through the same company.

This is not a good idea because if the consultancy side of the business collapses, then the creditors can call on the property assets in the business to settle any debts.

The consultancy directors would be better setting up a second company to buy investment property under a slightly different ownership structure to avoid associated company issues.

Extending ownership

Direct beneficial ownership of a property only permits four owners, but companies can extend that ownership by issuing shares.

The principle is simple: – the company owns a property but the rental profits and any chargeable gains are paid as dividends according to share ownership.

This flexibility spreads the risks and profits across more people.

Instead of individual owners gifting or selling part of a property to someone other than a spouse and triggering capital gains and stamp duty, issuing shares to another owner within a company accomplishes the same result without the tax issues.

Deciding If A Company Is For You

Owning property with a company can mean balancing the non-tax benefits like limited liability and extending ownership as discussed in the previous section with the tax pros and cons.

That common question introduced at the start of the chapter about as to whether to own letting property personally or with a company has no right or wrong answer.

Each investor needs to consider the personal issues involved in switching to a corporate structure.

Here are some important points to consider when making the decision to start a company, but do not forget this is not an exhaustive list and many other personal and business factors might come into play.

Standard tax rates

The old problem of companies paying tax on profits at a higher rate than an individual pays income tax was removed by Chancellor George Osborne equalising corporation tax rates with the basic rate of income tax across successive Budgets

Companies pay tax at 20% on the first £300,000 of profits – the same as basic rate taxpayers would pay but considerably less than the rates paid by higher (40%) and top rate (45%) taxpayers.

See How Companies Tax Income on Page 270

Indexation relief

Companies pay do not pay capital gains tax like an individual property owner, but do have indexation relief, which removes inflation from property gains.

See How Companies Tax Gains on Page 273

Income shifting and tax mitigation

Holding profits in a company taxed at 20% and then releasing them as dividends to shareholders lets taxpayers choose when they draw income and pay the tax.

Individuals and joint owners must declare all their annual income and gains and pay tax according to the tax year when they receive the money.

This is a real benefit to higher rate taxpayers, who can save cash in a company and drip release the money at a later date to keep their tax bills down.

Basic rate taxpayers can also take larger shareholdings to use up their unused lower rate tax rate bandings

No personal reliefs

Capital gains tax principle residence relief for your main home is a valuable tax reducer, and companies miss out on this, along with the annual exempt amount, letting reliefs and Rent-A-Room allowances.

Private property use is a tax quagmire

If directors have private use of company assets, these are seen as benefits and are heavily taxed, whereas private use of a property is sometimes a benefit to an individual – like PRR as a capital gains reducer.

Companies are a pain to run

Companies take up more time and cost more money to run because they are regulated by Companies House and are closely monitored by HMRC.

Besides keeping a company register and updating Companies House about any changes regularly, the accounts are more detailed and filed publicly, so outsiders can view your financial affairs.

Companies also have to file tax returns - and so do directors and shareholders receiving any income or dividends.

Because of the more complicated accounts and tax computations, companies also cost more to run – between £1,000 and £1,500 a year plus VAT.

Property Management Companies

Property management companies do not own any rental property but act as your letting agent - and they can also manage property for other landlords.

The company handles maintenance and manages tenants. That includes collecting the rent and paying the bills.

One way of seeing how a property management company can save tax is by following a worked example:

George is a higher rate taxpayer and owns four buy to let properties that generate rental profits of around £30,000. His tax on rents is £30,000 x 40%, which is £12,000.

George sets up a management company to look after the portfolio and pays the company 15% of the annual letting income to manage the properties.

That means George diverts around £4,500 of his profits into the company as the management fee, which reduces the rental profits to £25,500.

The company pays corporation tax at 20% on the £4,500 fee, which is £900. George would have paid tax £1,800 tax on the fee, so saves £900 in tax, providing he does not draw the money as a dividend.

Calculating whether the management company saves tax involves factoring the costs of incorporating and running the company into your financial model. If the company costs more to run than the amount of tax it is saving, then it is doubtful whether incorporating is worthwhile.

Associated companies

These complicated rules are due to be abolished in April 2015. They were introduced so individuals and companies could not split businesses to take advantage of more beneficial tax rates for some of their profits.

Now the basic rate income tax and corporation tax rates align at 20%, the problem has evaporated.

Nevertheless, governments have a habit of having yo-yo corporate tax rates, so consider the impact of increased tax rates if you are thinking about incorporation.

Action List

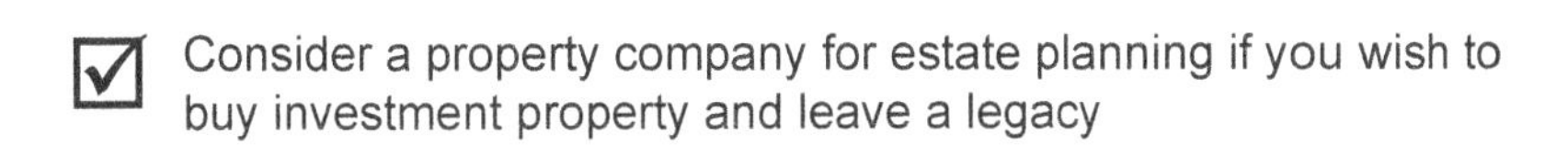

Consider a property company for estate planning if you wish to buy investment property and leave a legacy

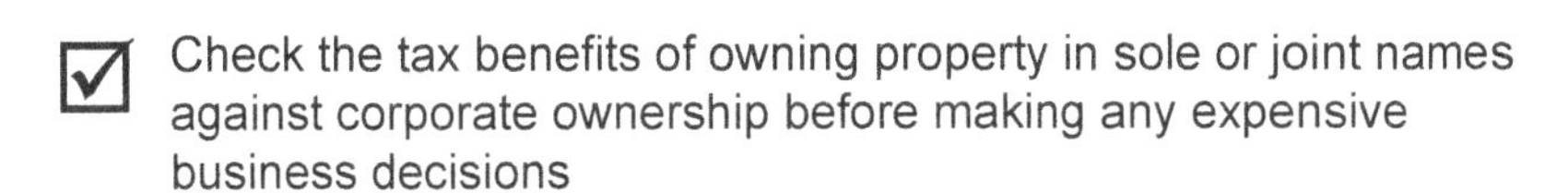

Check the tax benefits of owning property in sole or joint names against corporate ownership before making any expensive business decisions

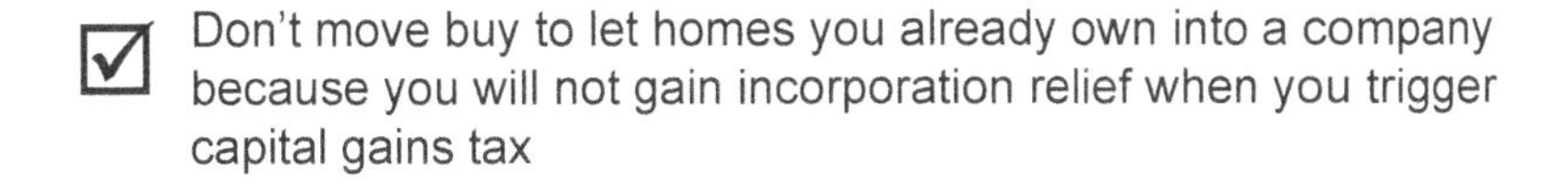

Don't move buy to let homes you already own into a company because you will not gain incorporation relief when you trigger capital gains tax

Chapter 21

Stacking Up A Property Deal

Chapter preview:

- Working out return on investment
- What yield tells property investors
- Rent cover for mortgages
- Explaining loan-to-value
- Setting your budget from a deposit
- Comparing buy to let mortgages

Before considering property tax, landlords have to make some important financial decisions as to whether a property deal is worth the time and money.

To help with these decisions, professional landlords will often draw on some simple formulas as indicators of potential rental profits.

It's a good idea to run through these three simple calculations before committing to a property deal.

Working Out Return On Investment

Return on investment or yield is the money a landlord can expect to receive against the capital invested in a property. Yield is expressed as a percentage. The larger the number, the better the return on investment.

To make any sense of the number, landlords need to identify

some base figure for property investment yields. However, the catch is no one publishes any such figure and yield can even vary between identical properties on the same street.

This is why you need to know how to work out the figures out for yourself.

Some estate agents and property portals publish average yields by region from time to time.

The historical average yield is 5% gross, so this is the benchmark. If your figures is lower than this, then the return is less than the market average.

Rental yield comes as two figures – gross and net yields.

Calculating gross rental yield

Gross yields are simply the rental return divided by the property value.

For example, if the monthly rent on a property with a value of £170,000 is £750, then:

- Multiply the monthly rent by 12 to give the annual rent, ie £750 x 12 = £9,000
- Divide the annual rent by the property value, ie £9,000 divided by £170,000 = 0.0529
- Multiply 0.0529 by 100 to give a gross rental yield of 5.29%

Calculating net rental yield

The net rental yield is a similar calculation to working out the gross yield, but the running costs of the property are also included.

So, for the net figure, take the annual rent and subtract annual running costs, such as mortgage interest, insurance, letting costs, repairs and maintenance etc.

Then divide the figure by property value and multiply the result by 100 to give the net yield.

What Yield Tells Property Investors

Use the yield to work out what the property is worth as an investment. For example, if research shows that the average rent to expect for a similar property in a reasonable rental state in the neighbourhood is £650 a month, then that's the starting point for calculating the value to an investor.

Take the average rental yield for a property in the area by working out the gross yield from the average rent for flats, terraced houses or semi-detached houses in the neighbourhood.

If a property is returning less than 5% a year on investment, then it's probably not worth buying.

To find the gross yield divide the sale price by the yield and multiply by 100.

For example, the average home in the neighbourhood is selling for £155,000 and generating an average rent of £650 a month, which gives a gross yield of 5.2%.

However, the seller wants £175,000 but the landlord is unlikely to find a tenant willing to pay more than £650 a month rent.

That takes the gross yield down to 4.45%.

Just up the road is a similar home is selling for £145,000.

That takes the yield at a rent of £650 a month up to 5.4%.

Assuming the cheaper property does not need a huge refurbishment, the gross yield is a good indicator of whether a property is over or under priced.

Rent Cover For Mortgages

Rent cover is a phrase bandied about by mortgage lenders and brokers. The formula is a test to show whether the rent a property generates allows landlords to pay their mortgage interest and other bills.

In other words, rent cover is an affordability test applied to each investment mortgage application in the same way as an income test is applied to each residential mortgage.

The lender will require a percentage cover – somewhere around 125% to 130% of the monthly rental income.

In simple terms, take 100 from the figure and the percentage that's left is the excess over the mortgage interest payment the lender wants to see from the monthly rent.

So, rent cover of 125% means rent cover should equal the monthly interest-only mortgage payment plus 25%.

Typically, rent cover is calculated on an interest rate of 5%. Do check this with your lender as the figure can vary between banks and building societies and also changes from time-to-time.

Taking a £170,000 property generating a monthly rent of £750 bought with a £127,500 mortgage, if the lender wants rent cover of 125%, the calculation is:

- The mortgage amount multiplied by the lender's 'cover rate' divided by 12 – which is (£127,500 x 5%) divided by 12
- £127,500 x 5% = £6,375, which is the annual interest only mortgage repayment
- Convert this to a monthly mortgage repayment by dividing by 12, which comes to £531
- Find out what the monthly rent cover figure is by multiplying by 125%, which is the lender's rent cover in this case

  So that's £531 x 125% = £664

As that figure is less than the £750 monthly rent, the landlord can borrow the £127,500 without any problem.

Rent doesn't pass rent cover test

If the monthly rent was £495 a month, the figures would change significantly.

The rent cover needed to service the borrowing is still £664, but the rent is only £495. To work out the maximum borrowing, first multiply the rent by 12. That's £495 x 12 = £5,940 (the annual rent).

£5,940 is 125% rent cover, so the interest repayment the rent can service is £5,940 divided by 125%, or £4,752 (£396 a month).

That £4,752 represents 5% of the amount borrowed, because the interest rate is 5%, so divide by 5 and multiply by 100 to give the maximum mortgage available with an interest only repayment of £396 a month.

So, £4,752 divided by 5 is £950.40, multiplied by 100 is £95,040.

Now take the maximum loan-to-value offered by the lender, say 75% in this case, and £95,040 is 75% of the property value.

Add a deposit of 25%, which is £31,680, and the property value the rent will allow an investor to buy on a 75% mortgage is £126,720.

Applying the rent cover test

The rent cover test is not only protection for the lender's money, but should give a savvy investor some idea of whether they are paying over or under value for a property.

If the rent passes the rent cover test, then the lender will advance up to the maximum loan-to-value for the property.

If the affordability test is failed, then the maximum loan is set at the amount rent cover calculates as a sensible price for the property.

Explaining Loan To Value (LTV)

Loan-to-value is how much a mortgage lender is ready to lend against the value of a property.

Mortgage offers have a double indemnity clause in favour of the lender – the wording is always something like 'the mortgage advance is either a percentage of the purchase price or the valuation, whichever is the lowest'.

The idea is if the buyer agrees some foolish purchase price that is way over the market value, the lender will only offer an advance that is a strict percentage of the surveyor's valuation.

Loan-to-value is expressed as a percentage and often as the abbreviation 'LTV'.

When you see '75% LTV mortgage' that means the lender will advance the lowest of 75% of the purchase price or 75% of the surveyor's property valuation.

Setting Your Budget From A Deposit

To save wasting time chasing property that you can probably not afford to buy, here's a quick way to work out the maximum purchase price from the cash deposit you have available for a purchase.

First take the loan-to-value of the mortgage – say the average is 75%.

That means the lender will put up 75% of the property value, so you have to find the remaining 25% as a deposit.

To find the deposit from a property value with a 75% LTV mortgage, take the purchase price and divide by 25%, which is £170,000 x 25%, giving a £42,500 deposit.

Work the formula backwards to find out the price of a home you can buy with a deposit of £42,500 with a mortgage of 75% LTV.

That's £42,500 divided by 25 x 100 = £170,000.

Stress Testing Property Deals

The formulas in this chapter are regularly applied by professional investors, mortgage underwriters and surveyors to test buy to let affordability.

Without the tests, it's all too easy to put in an offer on a property that is not financially viable as a buy to let or house in multiple occupation.

Don't forget to put a margin in for refurbishment and working capital to cover the mortgage and other running costs that you will have to pay out of your own pocket before the first tenant moves in.

Comparing Buy To Let Mortgages

Buy to let lenders and brokers will say hundreds more buy to let mortgage deals are on the market compared to any other time.

They're right and wrong. Yes, more than 600 buy to let mortgage deals are available at the time of writing this book.

But those deals are often the same package rewrapped by marketers – for instance a two-year fixed rate may be available at 60% LTV, 75% and 80% LTV.

To marketers they are three different mortgage deals, but the reality is they are offering the same mortgage tweaked to look different to appeal to different types of borrowers.

The way mortgages work is that most lenders borrow their cash from similar sources at similar prices.

They then package this money to market to buy to let investors.

One fixed or tracker deal may have a low rate and high fees, while another may have no fees and a higher rate.

Comparing the market to find the best deal is a nightmare, but ignore the headline rate and look at the underlying monthly repayments and costs.

Here's a worked example comparing two fixed rate mortgages:

- Deal 1 is 1.99% at 60% LTV over 26 months with a £2,500 arrangement fee and a £99 booking fee at 4.9% APR
- Deal 2 is 2.20% at 60% LTV 0ver 24 months with a £895 arrangement fee and £99 booking fee at 4.8% APR. For the additional two months of the 26 month comparison, the mortgage reverts to 4.99%.

Deal 1	**£**	**£**
26 x £423.37 a month	11,007.62	
Arrangement fee	2,500.00	
Booking fee	99.00	
TOTAL		13,606.62
Monthly cost over 26 months		523.33

Deal 2		
24 x £433.66 a month	10,407.84	
2 x £572.41 (4.99% rate)	1,144.82	
Arrangement fee	895.00	
Booking fee	99.00	
TOTAL		12,546.66
Monthly cost over 26 months		482.56
Total saving on Deal 2		**1,060.02**

The moral is ignore the marketing wrapper and work out all the costs of a buy to let mortgage over the same period – 26 months in this case. Interest rates and APR mean little when fees are included in the deal.

Action List

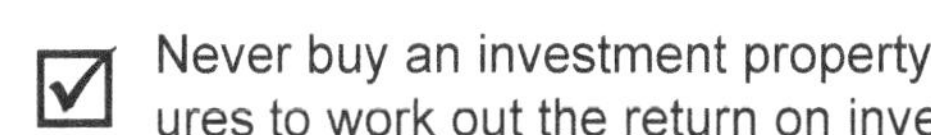

☑ Never buy an investment property on a whim - always run the figures to work out the return on investment to show that the home will make a profit

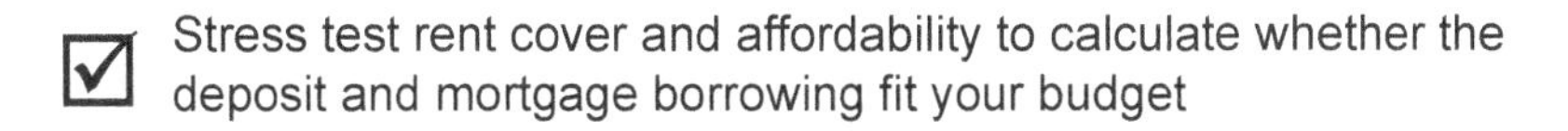

☑ Stress test rent cover and affordability to calculate whether the deposit and mortgage borrowing fit your budget

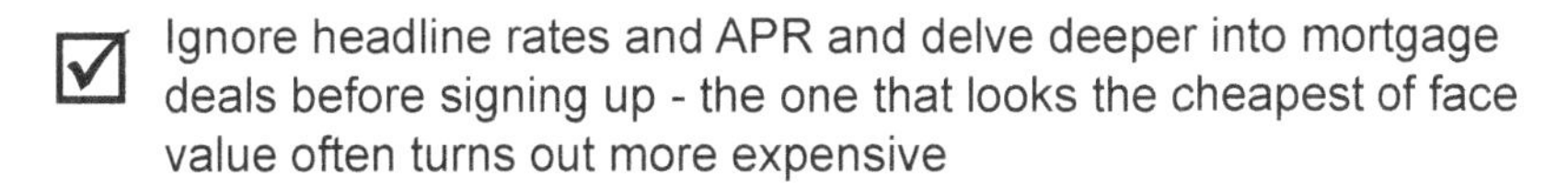

☑ Ignore headline rates and APR and delve deeper into mortgage deals before signing up - the one that looks the cheapest of face value often turns out more expensive

Chapter 22

Property Tax Flowcharts

Chapter preview:

- UK buy to let or HMOs
- UK or EEA Holiday Lets
- UK or overseas uncommercial lets
- Overseas buy to let or holiday lets
- UK buy to sell property

These flowcharts are quick guides to identifying which property business a property slots into and which tax return forms should be completed for rental income or on disposal of the property.

Just work down each flowchart level by level to see how to treat each property for tax. Each chart has the same headings in the left hand column.

First, select where the property is located.

Next, choose your intention for the property on purchase and your trading status as an individual, joint owner or company.

Once you have selected these options, the taxes you pay and the self-assessment tax forms that need completing each year become apparent.

The forms are available online at the HMRC web site - the link is http://search2.hmrc.gov.uk/kb5/hmrc/forms/selfassessmentforms.page

UK Buy To Let Tax Flowchart

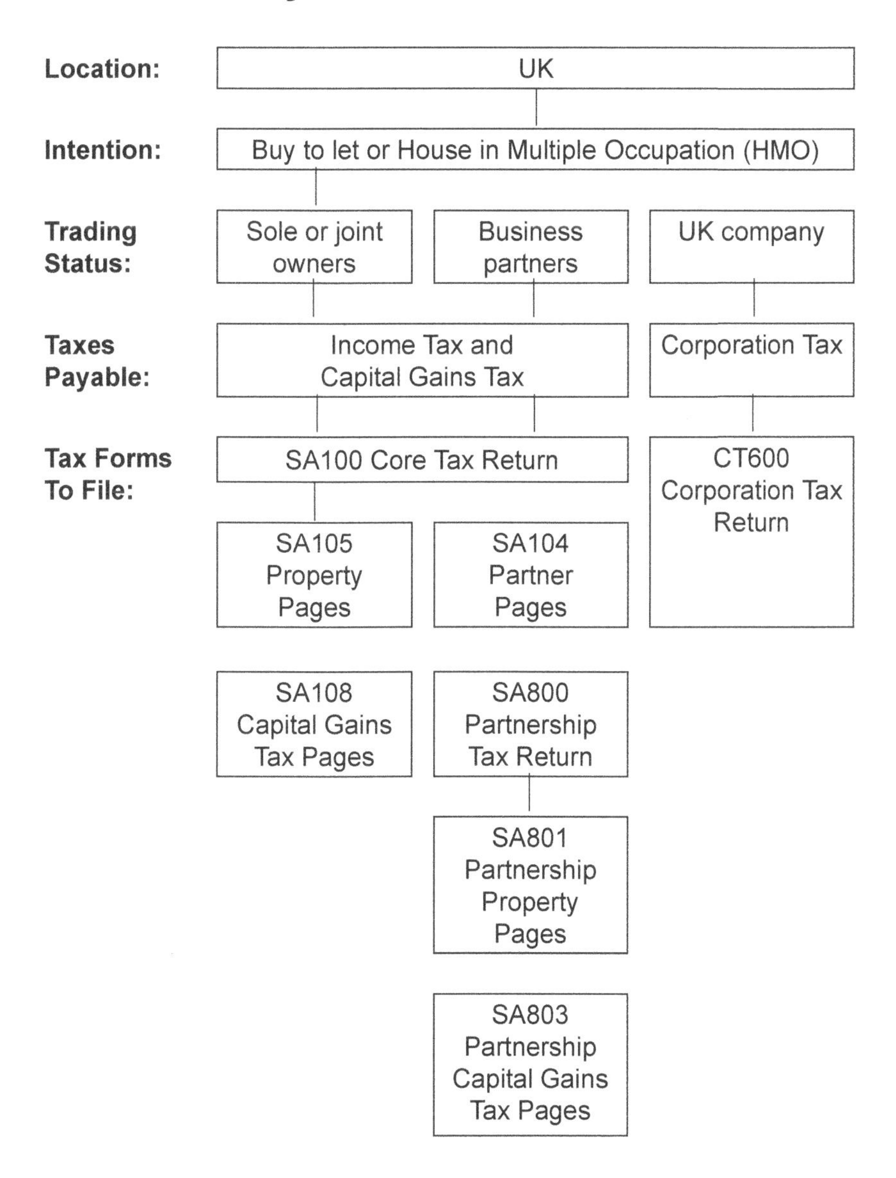

UK or EEA Holiday Let Tax Flowchart

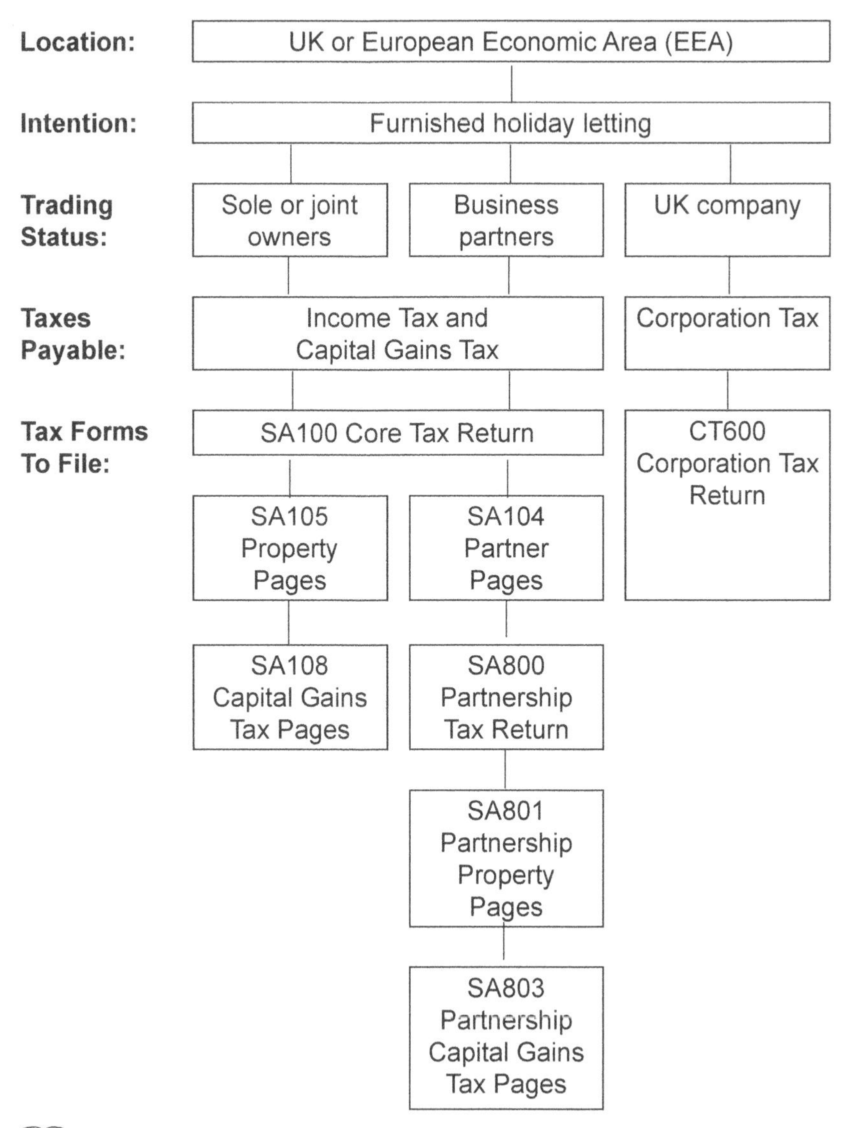

See Page 63 for a list of European Economic Area countries

UK Uncommercial Let Tax Flowchart

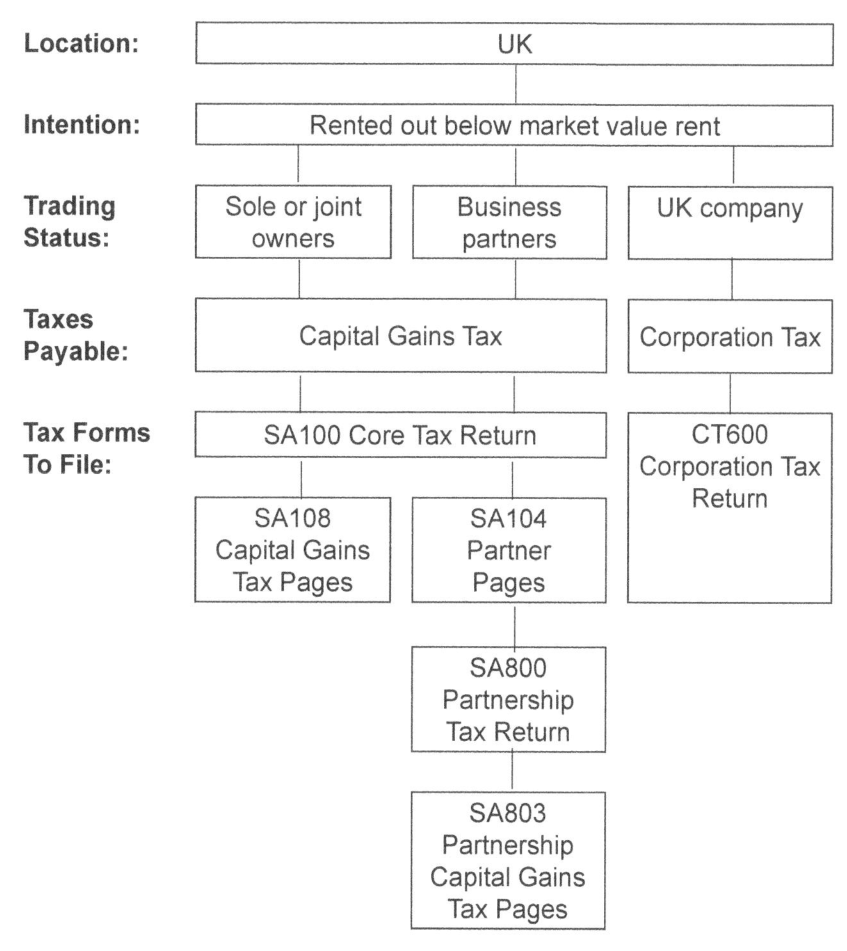

If the uncommercial letting property is outside the UK and tax has been paid on the gain overseas, also complete the SA106 Foreign Pages - See Page 242

Overseas Property Tax Flowchart

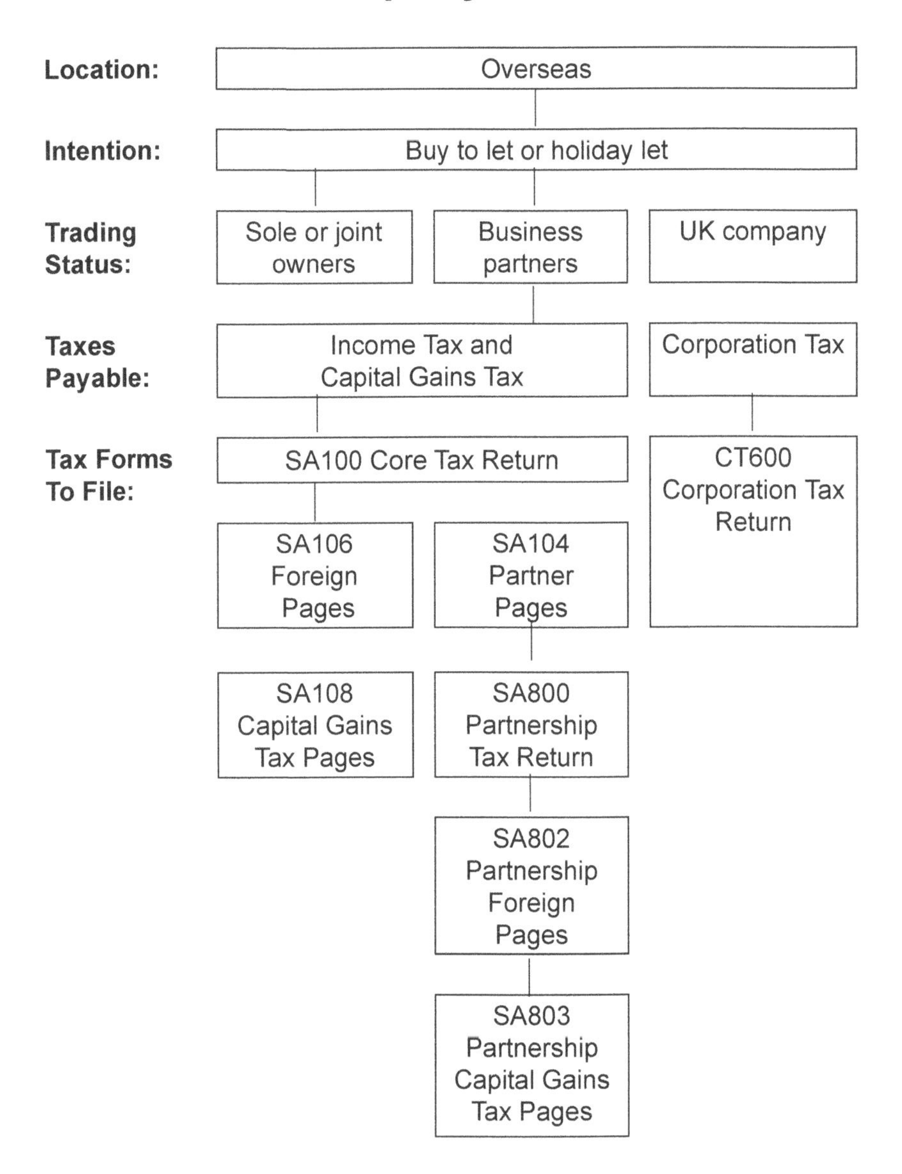

UK Buy To Sell Tax Flowchart

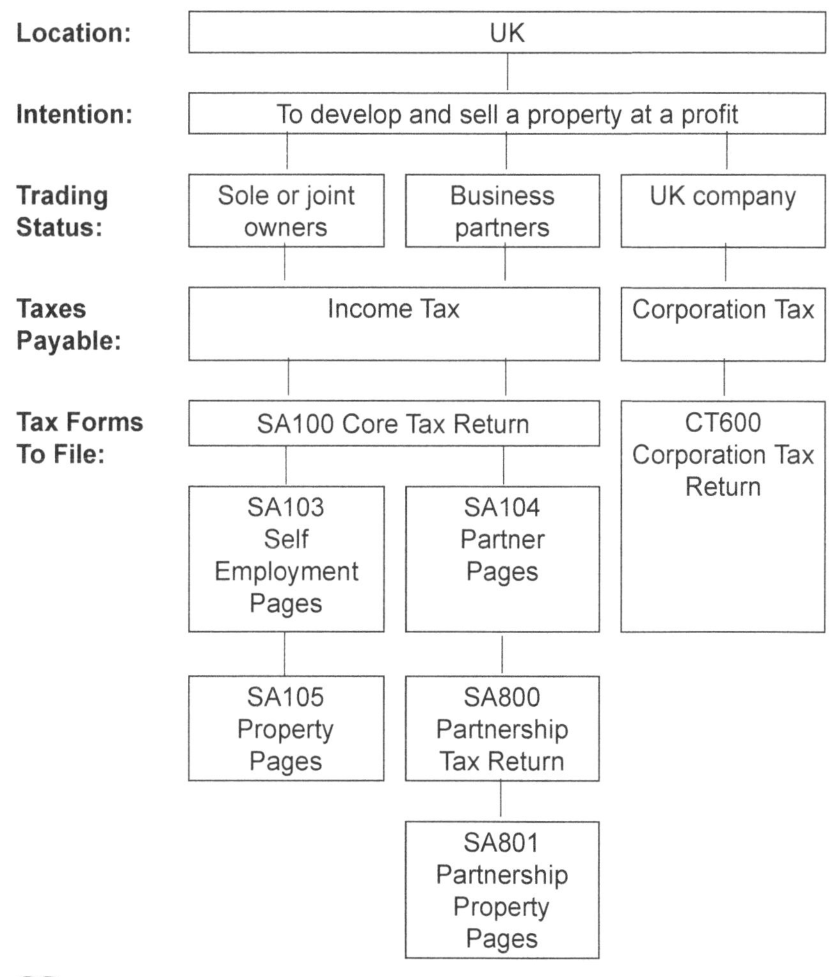

If the property is rented out pending sale, any rental income is declared on property pages in the same way buy to let landlords declare rents.

INDEX

A

B

INDEX

INDEX

D

E

F

INDEX

J

K

L

M

R

S

T

U

V

W

Lightning Source UK Ltd.
Milton Keynes UK
UKOW06f1150210715

255570UK00001B/1/P